UNDERCURRENTS · Series Editor Carol Coulter

Consent: Bridging the Gap between Doctor and Patient

MARY DONNELLY

CORK **cup** UNIVERSITY PRESS

First published in 2002 by
Cork University Press
University College
Cork
Ireland

British Library Cataloguing in Publication Data
A CIP catalogue record for this book is available from
the British Library

ISBN 1 85918 275 5

Typeset by Tower Books, Ballincollig, Co. Cork
Printed by ColourBooks, Baldoyle, Co. Dublin

Contents

Acknowledgements

I would like to thank the following people for help and inspiration, in many different forms, during my work on this pamphlet: Des Clarke, Carol Coulter, Dolores Dooley, Deirdre Madden, Brendan Mee, John Mee, Emily Spieler, Darius Whelan and the staff of Cork University Press.

Mary Donnelly

Introduction

The traditional Hippocratic Oath, sworn by generations of doctors,[1] requires the physician to 'prescribe regimen for the good of my patients according to my ability and my judgement and never do harm to anyone'. The patient's views as to what constituted her[2] good did not have to be canvassed.

Like many hitherto unexamined aspects of Irish society, the relationship between doctor and patient has been re-evaluated in recent years. In theory, at least, we now live in a society where patient, and not doctor, knows best and where an individual's informed consent is a fundamental prerequisite for any medical procedure. In the recently launched health strategy, *Quality and Fairness: A Health System for You*, a primary objective of the strategy is that the patient be placed at the centre in the delivery of care. Thus, the stated vision of the future healthcare system from the patient's perspective is one that 'encourages you to have your say, listens to you, and ensures your views are taken into account.'[3]

Yet in spite of the importance afforded to patient participation in medical decisions – in policy documents and by legal, ethical and medical commentators – the reality is that genuine and informed consent to medical procedures is often absent. Many of us, either by choice or because we have no alternative, still leave the responsibility for our healthcare decisions in the hands of our physicians. The aim of this pamphlet is to ask why this is the case and to consider how our healthcare system, and the legal framework that underpins it, must be developed in order to ensure that the patient is in a real sense placed at the centre of our healthcare system. In doing this, the pamphlet focuses on the principle of informed consent to medical procedures and argues that an understanding of this principle is essential if the objective of making the patient central is to be achieved.

The pamphlet begins in Chapter 1 by looking at the requirement for informed consent to medical procedures and shows that the ethical and legal principles we now take for granted are of comparatively recent origin. As recently as the 1990s, it would appear that Irish hospitals had permitted the removal and retention of organs from deceased children without either parental knowledge or consent.[4] This, and many other examples considered in Chapter 1, indicates that the idea of asking what a patient thinks about a medical procedure – or abiding by her wishes in this regard – is a relatively new one.

In Chapter 2 the pamphlet considers the principles that underpin the notion of consent and examines the importance of personal autonomy. Why do we feel invaded if subjected to medical procedures without our knowledge? Why should we be permitted to refuse medical treatment even if any rational observer would consider the decision to be foolish, selfish or downright mad? However, consent and the protection of patient autonomy is not just important in these extreme cases. Most of us simply want to make the most appropriate healthcare decision for our circumstances and, in order to do this, we wish to be informed of our options and consulted about which is the most suitable. Informed consent in this regard is merely a manifestation of the basic requirement for communication between doctor and patient, but with the added recognition that it is the patient who is making the decision.

In spite of the acknowledgement that obtaining the consent of the patient to medical treatment is a fundamental ethical principle, there is a considerable dissonance between informed consent as an ideal and the reality experienced by many patients. Chapter 3 explores this dissonance, looking first at the ethical ideal of informed consent. How much information should a patient have? How free from her doctor's influence and the influence of her family and friends should she be? Having established this ideal, it then falls to examine how the practice in Ireland measures up to the ideal. In order to do so, this chapter looks at the rights afforded to patients under the *Charter of Rights for Hospital Patients* and at the ethical standards of the medical profession found in the Irish Medical Council's *Guide to Ethical Conduct and Behaviour* (1998). It also examines patient surveys and sample consent forms to see how patients experience the requirement for consent in practice. This examination reveals that, while practices in this regard have undoubtedly improved in recent years, many patients still report very elementary omissions in this aspect of their healthcare.

The dissonance between the ideal of informed consent and the reality experienced by patients arises in no small way from the legal treatment of issues relating to consent. While the law has been crucial in the popularization of informed consent, the legal understanding of the concept is a much impoverished version of informed consent as an ideal. As a result, consent for many has become the functional equivalent of the consent form, a legal nicety to be complied with in order to protect the doctor from being sued. Chapter 4 critiques the contribution of the law in this area, exploring why it is that the law on informed consent as it currently operates can never deliver informed consent as an ideal.

The focus in the pamphlet until this point has been on how to protect individual autonomy and facilitate personal informed consent. However, this is only one half of the consent picture. The notions of informed consent and patient participation take on a different aspect where a patient is, temporarily or permanently, incapable of making a decision for herself. Thus, for young children, for people with serious learning difficulties, and for people with serious mental illness or dementia, personal consent is not possible and some form of proxy consent must be obtained. This does not mean that respect for individual autonomy is no longer relevant but that other concerns, including pre-eminently the welfare of the patient, must also be taken into account. Protecting the vulnerable patient in these situations is a legal and ethical responsibility and presents many challenges.

A first concern is how to distinguish between people who are competent to give personal consent and those who are not. Ensuring that this distinction is properly made is fundamental to the protection of patient autonomy: if the standard of competence is set too high, individuals are denied the opportunity to take control of their own healthcare decisions; if it is set too low, the individual's consent occurs in name only. Chapter 5 looks at how decisions about competence are made and sets out the factors which should be taken into account when making these decisions.

Once it is clear that a patient is incapable of giving her own personal consent, other ethical and legal issues arise. Two groups of patients may be distinguished. Children, in most cases, will have a parent or parents available to make decisions on their behalf. The issues with parental decision-making are examined in Chapter 6. How constrained are parents in this situation? Can parents refuse necessary medical treatment for their children on the basis of religious or other beliefs? The recent case before the Supreme Court where parents refused to permit their child to have the PKU (or heel) test shows that these questions are increasingly relevant in a multicultural society.[5] This chapter also emphasizes the importance of ensuring that parental consent is a fully informed consent and that parental participation in medical decision-making is facilitated.

The second group of patients who cannot give personal consent to medical treatment is that of adults who do not have the necessary legal competence to consent. Chapter 7 looks at the way in which these people have been treated by the law and in practice. This chapter argues that, although the recently introduced Mental Health Act 2001 does improve the position of some mentally ill people, a much more wide-ranging reform is required if we are to protect the welfare and the autonomy of the frequently vulnerable people in this position.

Having explored the realities facing Irish patients today, the pamphlet will conclude by looking at the strategic planning needed for the delivery of a more patient-centred healthcare system. Does the recently published Health Strategy contain the necessary policies to achieve its goal? What additional policy developments are required in order to move forward in this regard? The conclusion of this pamphlet is that a patient-centred healthcare system can only be achieved if we give due recognition to the concept of patient rights and acknowledge the centrality of patient autonomy.

1. Developing a Culture of Consent

Consent: A Recent Phenomenon

In a telling exchange at the Tribunal of Inquiry into the Contamination with HIV and Hepatitis C of Persons with Haemophilia and Related Diseases (more commonly known as the Lindsay Tribunal), Professor Ian Temperley (the former medical director of the National Haemophilia Treatment Centre) was asked why in 1983 he had not informed a woman that the new treatment he had prescribed for her haemophiliac son carried a risk of infection from AIDS.[1] He responded by saying that this was not the way things were done at that time – he had considered the situation carefully and made an informed decision to switch the boy from his existing treatment. Informing the boy's mother simply did not arise. Professor Temperley's behaviour was neither unique nor especially unusual. At the same tribunal, Professor Christine Lee, Director of the London Royal Free Hospital's Haemophilia Centre, confirmed that in the mid-1980s it was not the Centre's policy to discuss treatments with patients. However, like Professor Temperley, she noted 'times have changed'.[2]

As the above exchanges indicate, the requirement to obtain patient consent (or that of the patient's parents if a child is involved) is a modern phenomenon as is the accompanying focus on providing information. The history of medical interventions and medical research is rich with examples of research and medical procedures carried out without consent. These range from situations of blatant disregard for the patient through to paternalistic assumptions about the patient's welfare. What is striking about most of these examples, some of which are discussed below, is that the behaviour in question was considered perfectly legitimate by society at that time. In other words, the medical or scientific communities did not act alone in proceeding to treatment without consent but were enthusiastically supported in this attitude by legal and societal attitudes.

Disregarding the Patient

The collaboration between the law and the medical and social services professions in disregarding the patient's consent may be seen in the decision of the US Supreme Court in *Buck* v *Bell* (1927). Carrie Buck was, in the language of the time, 'feeble-minded'.[3] The daughter of a mentally disabled mother, she had been committed to an institution in 1924 when she was 17-years-old. Prior to this time, she had given birth to a daughter who was described to the court (incorrectly[4]) as being 'of defective mentality'. The manager of the institution decided to have Carrie sterilized to prevent any further pregnancies. Carrie understood what was proposed, objected to the sterilization and brought her case ultimately to the US Supreme Court. The Court held that the sterilization was lawful and Justice Oliver Wendell Holmes, perhaps the leading American jurist of the twentieth century, justified the procedure on the following basis:

> It is better for all the world, if instead of waiting to execute degenerate offspring for crime, or to let them starve for their imbecility, society can prevent those who are manifestly unfit from continuing their kind. The principle that sustains compulsory vaccination is broad enough to cover cutting the fallopian tubes . . . Three generations of imbeciles is enough.[5]

What is startling about this judgment is not Justice Holmes' reliance on a scientifically inaccurate eugenics theory. (At this time, belief in eugenics was widespread. By 1937, thirty-one of the states in the US had passed compulsory sterilization statutes and countless women and men were sterilized without their consent.[6]) Instead, what is extraordinary is that a judge known for his concern for the rights of individuals – and operating within the United States Constitution which guarantees individual rights – could not see that forcing a woman to have a sterilization without her consent could be a violation of her rights. In the same way, in Sweden, a country famed as a liberal bastion, governmental policy resulted in the compulsory steril-ization of up to 63,000 people, most of whom were women, between 1936 and 1976. Many of these women were mentally ill, mentally disabled or epileptic, while others were released from prison, were poor or alcoholic. Although many of the women had signed consent forms, there were strong indications that they had either not understood what they were consenting to, or had been forced to sign as a condition of prison release, or in order to obtain welfare benefits or retain custody of their chil-dren. The notion that this procedure was impermissible without the genuine consent of the women was simply not recognized.[7]

The collaboration between medical and legal bodies in disre-garding patients may be seen, less dramatically, in an Irish context in the Supreme Court's decision in *Daniels* v *Heskin* (1954). Here, the Court considered whether a doctor should have informed a woman, who was suffering from post-partum discomfort, that a needle had remained in her body following stitching after childbirth. A majority of the Court rejected the notion of a general duty to disclose information to patients. Justice Kingsmill Moore argued that '[a]ll depends on the circum-stances – the character of the patient, her health, her social position, her intelligence . . . and innumerable other considera-tions.'[8] The notion of a patient having a right to know was not even considered.

Disregarding the Research Subject

Most of the medical developments we take for granted have been built upon scientific experimentation on human subjects. Although to modern eyes it may appear obvious that special care should be taken to obtain the consent of individuals who are to act as the subjects of research, this attitude is also relatively new. A brief examination of one of the most infamous experi-ments[9] (outside of those carried out by Nazi physicians[10]) in medical history indicates how scientists and society can conspire to disregard the research subject. The Tuskegee Syphilis Study was carried out by the United States Public Health Service to investigate the pathological evolution of syphilis if left untreated. Beginning in 1932 and continuing until 1972, 399 poor black sharecroppers in Macon County, Alabama, who had latent syphilis were routinely observed to see how their condition developed. The men were not told the nature of their condition, being told only that they had 'bad blood'. They were denied any form of treatment or therapy and the researchers took steps to ensure that they would not obtain treatment elsewhere. They were persuaded to subject themselves to invasive and painful research procedures on the basis that the procedures were 'special free treatment'. They were rewarded for their participation in the experiment by the provision of free meals and burial insurance. On 16 May 1997, President Clinton apologized to the eight survivors and to the broader African-American community for the harms done to them by the experiment. In his words, '[t]he United States government did something that was wrong – deeply, profoundly, morally wrong. It was an outrage to our commitment to integrity and equality for all our citizens.' [11]

While nothing of this nature has emerged in an Irish context, concerns have been raised about a number of medical trials carried out in the 1960s and 1970s. Three trials were carried out to investigate the efficiency of vaccines for common childhood illnesses. As part of these trials, a total of 211 children were vaccinated, about half of whom were resident in children's homes. Although the physician involved did state that she obtained the consent of parents where the children were resident with their parents or where mothers specifically requested information, there is no indication in the trial reports or the subsequent journal articles that consent was regarded as an issue in relation to the children who were in residential care. A report carried out by the Department of Health (and released in November 2000)[12] could not conclude on whether consent to the trials had been given. The Minister for Health, Mícheál Martin, has referred the matter to the Laffoy Commission to Inquire into Child Abuse Against Children in the Care of the State with the comment that there was not evidence that 'solid informed consent' had been obtained.[13]

Although the Tuskagee Syphilis Trial and the Irish Vaccine Trials are vastly different in terms of the harm suffered by the subjects[14] and the behaviour of the researchers, the examples of both trials indicate the broad societal acceptance of experimentation without consent. The Tuskagee Syphilis Trial was well-documented – it was reviewed several time by officials from the US Public Health Services and reported in thirteen articles in prestigious journals. Similarly, the Irish Vaccine Trials were reported in international medical journals, and the medical officers and administrators of the children's homes were involved and aware of the procedures. Worrying about the niceties of consent (or about recording the fact that consent had actually been obtained) was simply not the way things were done at that time.

The picture painted above suggests an almost impenetrable barrier of societal indifference to issues relating to patient consent. This is not entirely true. The failure to obtain meaningful consent has always been most closely associated with disadvantaged members of society, disabled people, racial minorities, children, and people with fewer economic or educational resources. The affluent and the educated were less likely to be disregarded in relation to consent and, at any rate, were less likely to find themselves involved in drug trials or involuntary procedures. However, even the affluent and the educated are vulnerable when they are ill. For these people too, treatment without consent was a reality arising frequently from well-meaning assumptions made by members of the medical profession and endorsed by society. The accepted wisdom was that because doctors knew more about medical matters, they were in a better position than the patient to know what was in the patient's best interests. This meant that giving the patient the information necessary in order to make consent meaningful (namely, the information required to make a choice), was simply not an option.

Developing a Culture of Consent

The second half of the twentieth century saw a decisive shift in attitudes towards individual rights and especially towards the protection of individual autonomy. One crucial aspect of this shift was the development of a culture of consent in relation to medical treatment and experimentation. There are a number of reasons for this. First, the years after the Second World War saw widespread revulsion at the harms done in the name of medicine and science by Nazi physicians and this led the international community to take steps in order to prevent recurrences. The Nuremberg Code was adopted in 1947 and was substantially supplemented by the Helsinki Declaration of the World Medical Organisation 1964. Under these international instruments, the consent (and safety) of the research subjects was made central to all future experiments. Secondly, this era saw increasing challenges to authority. The civil rights campaigns in the United States and in Northern Ireland, the women's rights movement, and even the rise of consumer rights all placed emphasis on the individual's conflict with those traditionally invested with authority by society. It was inevitable that these challenges would extend to the medical profession. Thirdly, after almost two millennia of minding its own business, the law started to become involved in the relationship between doctor and patient. Although the effects of this involvement have not always been positive, it is indisputable that the law has been instrumental in moving consent, or, at any rate, the legal conception of consent, to centre stage.

Legal Recognition of Consent

Medico-legal historians cite the decision in *Slater* v *Baker and Stapleton* (1767) as the first time that the requirement to obtain a patient's consent to medical intervention was recognized by the courts. The plaintiff in this case hired the defendant doctors to remove bandages from his fractured leg. In spite of the plaintiff's protests, the doctors re-fractured the leg and placed it in an experimental brace to stretch it while the new fracture healed. The doctors were held to have acted improperly because 'a patient should be told what is about to be done to him, that he may take courage and put himself in such a situation as to enable him to undergo the operation.'[15] It was not, however, until 1914 in the foundational American case of *Schloendorff* v *Society of New York Hospital* that consent began to assume a position of real importance in the legal treatment of medical issues. In this case, the patient had agreed to have an abdominal examination under anaesthetic but had stipulated that there be 'no operation'. When the surgeon discovered a fibroid tumour during the course of the examination, he removed the tumour. In what is probably the most frequently quoted passage in medico-legal discourse, Justice Cardozo noted that:

> [E]very human being of adult years and sound mind has a right to determine what shall be done with his own body; and a surgeon who performs an operation without his patient's consent commits an assault for which he is liable in damages.[16]

Consent and its companions, autonomy and self-determination, had taken their places in the legal canon.

The importance of the principle encapsulated by Justice Cardozo in *Schloendorff* goes beyond mere actions for battery.[17] If the performance of an operation without the patient's consent is an assault, it is axiomatic that a patient's refusal to give his consent must be respected. Thus, as confirmed by courts in many countries, in all but the most exceptional circumstances an individual has the right to refuse medical treatment. This right to refuse extends even to situations where the treatment is necessary to save the life of the patient. In the words of Justice O'Flaherty in the decision of the Irish Supreme Court in *In Re a Ward of Court* (1995) 'there is an absolute right in a competent person to refuse medical treatment even if it leads to death'.[18]

In spite of the dramatic import of Justice Cardozo's statement, there was not an immediate flourishing of legal actions for non-consensual operations.[19] Instead, the locus for consent-related actions changed, with the increasing realization that consent in the absence of information about what is involved in the procedure is effectively meaningless. Thus, knowledge came to be seen as a fundamental prerequisite for a valid consent. In the US case of *Salgo* v *Leland Stanford Jr. University Board of Trustees* (1957), the term 'informed consent' was first used in order to express this more sophisticated concept. Martin Salgo became permanently paralysed following a surgical procedure. His physicians were held liable for breaching a duty (previously unrecognized) to disclose 'any facts which are necessary to form the basis of an intelligent consent by the patient to proposed treatment'.[20] Although important for establishing the concept of informed consent, *Salgo* is short on legal analysis. It was not until the decision of the District of Columbia Circuit Court of Appeals in *Canterbury* v *Spence* (1972) that the real foundations for the requirement for informed consent to medical procedures were laid. The powerful reasoning of Justice Robinson has compensated for the relatively lowly status of the Court and resulted in one of the most widely cited decisions in modern legal jurisprudence. Like *Salgo*, the plaintiff in *Canterbury* suffered permanent paralysis following a laminectomy, an operation carried out to relieve severe back pain. His surgeon had not told him that this operation carried a 1 per cent risk of paralysis. Quoting Justice Cardozo in *Schloendorff*, the Court in *Canterbury* held that:

> True consent to what happens to one's self is the informed exercise of a choice, and that entails an opportunity to evaluate knowledgeably the options available and the risks attendant upon each. The average patient has little or no understanding of the medical arts, and ordinarily has only his physician to whom he can look for enlightenment with which to reach an intelligent decision. From these almost

axiomatic considerations springs the need, and in turn
the requirement, for a reasonable divulgence by physician to patient to make such a decision possible.[21]

The basic legal principle established in *Canterbury*, namely that a
physician has a duty to disclose information about a procedure,
has now been accepted in most jurisdictions worldwide. It is not
an absolute principle. The Court in *Canterbury* recognized that a
doctor retains a 'therapeutic privilege' not to provide information to a patient if he believes that the disclosure of the
information would result in a serious deterioration in the
patient's condition or would render the patient incapable of
making a rational decision. However, as the Court recognized,
therapeutic privilege must be exercised with care:

> The [therapeutic privilege] exception obtains [if] risk
> disclosure poses such a threat of detriment to the
> patient as to become unfeasible or contraindicated from
> a medical point of view. It is recognized that patients
> occasionally become so ill or emotionally distraught on
> disclosure as to foreclose a rational decision, or compli-
> cate or hinder the treatment, or perhaps even pose
> psychological damage to the patient.[22]

2. The Principles Underpinning Consent

Underpinning the requirement for consent is the view that
people should have the right to make decisions for themselves.
Described alternately as the individual's right to autonomy or
self-determination, this view originates in the philosophy of the
Enlightenment.[1] In *In Re a Ward of Court* (1995), the right to self-
determination and the right to autonomy were confirmed by the
Supreme Court to be among the unspecified, personal rights
recognized by Article 40.3.1 of the Irish Constitution and arising
from the 'Christian and democratic' nature of the State. The
Court relied on the individual's right of autonomy, together with

a long list of other rights, to justify the cessation of life-sustaining treatment (in this case, hydration and nutrition) to a woman who had suffered irreversible brain damage 23 years previously. As a result of this, she was in a near-persistent vegetative state (or near-PVS)[2] where she had lost all communicative capacity and had probably also lost all cognitive capacity.[3] Outside of stating the rights, however, the Court had little to say about what a right to self-determination or autonomy actually meant.

The Concept of Autonomy

Deriving its origins from the Greek 'auto' (self) and 'nomos' (rule or law), closer examination of the concept of autonomy reveals that there is no single view of what is meant by autonomy. Although the term is used frequently, its use is rarely accompanied by any consideration of what the term actually means. Understanding the concept in a medical context is further complicated by the fact that many autonomy theorists have developed their ideas in the context of political theory where the autonomy in question is that of the State or of the individual in relation to the State.

There are two broadly opposing views of what autonomy means. One's approach to the question of consent will be dependent on which view of autonomy one adopts. The first view is indicated in the following passage by the philosopher Isaiah Berlin:

> I wish to be an instrument of my own, not of other men's, acts of will. I wish to be a subject, not an object; to be moved by reasons, by conscious purposes, which are my own, not by causes which affect me, as it were, from outside. I wish to be somebody, not nobody; a doer – deciding, not being decided for, self-directed and not acted upon by external nature or by other men as if I were a thing, or an animal, or a slave incapable of playing a human role, that is, of conceiving goals and policies of my own and realizing them.[4]

Under this view, independence, self-sufficiency, and freedom from external influences and obligations are seen as the essential components of an autonomous individual. It is a view of the rugged individualist which has great appeal to the American psyche in particular and is exemplified in popular culture in the persona of John Wayne. It is also a view of autonomy that is unattainable for most people. Very few of us can be free, at all times in our lives, from external influences and still fewer of us would wish to conceive our goals and policies entirely on our own. This view of autonomy is also, as Gerald Dworkin[5] argues, inconsistent with other important values we hold, namely the values of 'loyalty, objectivity, commitment, benevolence, and love'.

Other theorists espouse a less individualist form of autonomy. Dworkin, who is representative of this position, argues that autonomy is 'the capacity of a person critically to reflect upon, and then attempt to accept or change, his or her preferences, desires, values, and ideals'.[6] Autonomy does not require independence for its own sake; an individual may be autonomous and still be receptive to, and indeed reliant on, the views of others provided that she does not accept these views unquestioningly but engages with them critically. It is only if we view autonomy in this way that it becomes possible to accommodate autonomy within a broader framework of values. For Dworkin, autonomy is only one of the values that should underpin our lives (and by extension our decision-making). He argues that:

> Autonomy *is* important, but so is the capacity for sympathetic identification with others, or the capacity to reason prudentially, or the virtue of integrity. Similarly, although it is important to respect the autonomy of others, it is also important to respect their welfare, or their liberty, or their rationality.[7]

The distinction between the strong, individualist view of autonomy and the weak, receptive view is of more than academic interest in the context of medical decision-making. This may be seen if we ask the question: can a person who says to her doctor or her friend or family 'I trust you totally to make my medical decisions for me' be viewed as autonomous? Under the first view of autonomy, the answer must be no. The individual must make her own independent decisions and cannot cede her right to do so. Thus, autonomy is not just a right, it is also a duty. Under this view of autonomy, the patient who asks 'What would you do, doctor?' has already ceded too much decision-making power. The doctor who responds other than by telling the patient that she must make her own decision is encroaching too closely on the patient's autonomy.

Under the second view of autonomy, a person can cede decision-making power and still be regarded as autonomous: '[s]omeone who wishes to be the kind of person who does whatever the doctor orders is as autonomous as the person who wants to evaluate those orders for himself.'[8] The point is that the autonomous individual has chosen for herself the course of action she wishes to pursue. The defining factor is her freedom to choose even if this choice is to cede her own authority.

The view of autonomy taken in this pamphlet is focused on individual freedom of choice rather than independence. While the focus on independent decision-making has some advantages (for example, it is a more decisive antidote to paternalistic tendencies in the medical profession), it is an inaccurate representation of most patients' realities. As Carl Schneider illustrates in his important study of patient preferences about autonomy, although the vast majority of patients want to be kept informed about their medical condition, many patients do not want to be the sole decision-maker in medical matters. This, he notes, is especially true in the case of elderly patients and patients who are very ill.[9] A focus on freedom of choice facilitates a view of autonomy that is more representative of patients' needs. Under this view of autonomy, ultimately a patient can decide not to decide herself but to rely on others to a greater or lesser extent. However, this decision can only be regarded as autonomous if the patient has been made aware of what her decision entails (and that it is in fact a decision). The question of what is required for freedom of choice to be meaningful will be explored in Chapter 3.

The Importance of Autonomy

If we take autonomy to mean freedom of choice, there are a number of reasons why it should provide a fundamental value for the relationship between doctor and patient. The first is summed up in the rather obvious question 'whose body is it?'[10] Who is more appropriate to make a decision about what should happen to one's body? For even the most conscientious doctor, the consequence of the decision will be a third-party conse-quence. For the patient, it will impact hugely on her ongoing, lived reality. For this reason, the immediacy of the patient's involvement makes her the obvious decision-maker. This in no way denies the importance of the doctor's expertise but it acknowledges that the patient is an expert too in relation to how she lives her life and the consequences and risks she is prepared to take.

There are also more immediately practical reasons why a focus on patient autonomy is important. All the evidence points to the fact that the vast majority of patients want to know the nature of their illness. Thus, in one survey, 96 per cent of patients stated that they would wish to know if their illness was cancer.[11] Recent studies show that this is the case even with patients who had traditionally been thought to prefer not to know the nature of their condition. In one recently published survey, 88 per cent of elderly patients stated that they would wish to know the nature of their illness even if the illness was cancer.[12]

Greater patient involvement may have therapeutic benefits for the patient. Research indicates that where patients have had an active involvement in deciding upon their treatment, the treatment may have a higher level of effectiveness. Thus, patients with hypertension benefited from having an active role in their treatment while patients with diabetes who had been involved in their treatment discussions achieved greater blood sugar control.[13] Patients with breast cancer have also been shown to suffer less depression and anxiety if they are more actively consulted in making treatment decisions.[14] Some research ascribes these benefits to the relationship between psychological processes and the central nervous and immune systems (known as the psychoneuroloimmunology theory). The more control an individual has over her situation, the less stressful she will find it, which in turn will lead to an enhanced immune function. Although this theory has not been proven, it remains the subject of ongoing research.[15] More indisputable is the claim that a patient who has been involved in a decision-making process is more likely to comply with a prescribed medical regime and therefore to achieve the maximum benefits from a course of treatment.

Patient involvement also has the benefit of allowing treatment to be directed to the specific needs of the patient. The fact that a patient is breast feeding, frequently has to drive long distances, or has sporadic but short work pressures are examples of the non-medical factors that may influence the appropriateness of treatment. Without patient involvement, this vital information is simply not available and treatment decisions are impoverished as a result.

As many aspects of medical practice, especially those involving hospitalization, become more specialized, patients may find themselves under the care of a range of medical professionals, each with their own area of expertise. Even within a single consultant's 'team', there will be a number of people responsible for delivering care and making treatment decisions. While greater specialization does bring many benefits, it also increases the risks of decisions being reached without taking account of all the relevant medical, not to mention non-medical, factors. Sometimes, the only person with a comprehensive view of what is happening is the patient. Involving the patient taps into this resource. Greater patient involvement, in this and other contexts, may also prevent medical errors. An involved patient may notice discrepancies, inaccuracies and omissions in medical treatment which can occur with even the most careful practitioner. The therapeutic benefits of avoiding accidents are obvious.

For medical professionals too there are benefits from greater patient involvement. The doctor is freed from the burdens (as well as the powers) of solitary decision-making. From a more self-interested point of view also, medical professionals can take comfort in the fact that an accident avoided is a negligence suit averted. Even if something does go wrong, patients who have been more involved in their own care decisions may be less likely to sue. Many patients who have taken legal actions say they do so because they want answers and, in some cases, apologies. Although greater respect for patient autonomy will not stop all negligence actions, the patient who has been closely involved in her treatment and who regards her doctor as a partner may be more reluctant to take legal action against her.

Limitations on Autonomy

It is important to be aware of the limitations of autonomy-focused arguments. Like any right, the right to autonomy is not absolute. In Ireland, certain choices are simply not available. Thus, the right to autonomy does not entitle a person to choose to end her own life and to be assisted by her doctor in doing so,[16] nor does it allow a woman to choose to terminate a pregnancy unless her life is in danger.[17] A choice may also be overridden in certain circumstances. For example, it is ethically and legally acceptable in some instances to require an individual who may have an infectious disease to subject herself to testing in order to protect public health.[18] Other interests may also be relevant. The classic case of the pregnant woman who refuses to consent to a medically recommended Caesarean section raises the question (especially in the Irish context) of whether foetal rights should outweigh the woman's right to autonomy.[19]

Choices are limited too for other kinds of reasons. Freedom of choice is less meaningful in a healthcare system where lack of funding limits the options available. Concerns about patient consent may seem like an unnecessary luxury while patients languish on waiting lists unable to give consent to procedures that simply are not happening. Similarly, one might ask whether it is meaningful to describe a patient who must make difficult treatment decisions as having any real choice in the matter. A patient quoted by Schneider illustrates the point effectively:

> When I went into the doctor's office after the first round of chemotherapy and said that I couldn't do it anymore, couldn't take any more needles or IVs, is that exercising autonomy? I was saying that I was giving up, just let me die. I sure didn't feel very autonomous. I didn't feel as if either of the choices I saw available were acceptable.[20]

It is indisputable that, when we are very ill, most of our options are not attractive. Respecting patient autonomy does not cure serious illnesses. Nor will it provide resources where none existed before. However, within the inevitable limits imposed by patients' situations, respect for patients' autonomy remains of central importance; not because it solves patients' problems but because it recognizes their fundamental human value.

3. Informed Consent: The Ideal and The Reality

Referring the Department of Health Report on Vaccine Trials to the Laffoy Commission,[1] Mícheál Martin, the Minister for Health and Children, expressed concerns about the possible absence of 'solid informed consent'. The fact that the Minister did not feel any need to define what he meant by this indicates the extent to which the term 'informed consent' has entered our lexicon. Yet, like many commonly accepted terms, it does not yield its meaning easily. Understanding informed consent requires a distinction to be made between informed consent as an ethical ideal and informed consent as a legal proposition.[2] Used in its non-legal context, the term informed consent is a shorthand for the amalgam of requirements which make consent to medical treatment meaningful. Thus, informed consent implies a choice made by a patient who is capable of making a choice, who has had sufficient information to understand what this choice means and who is not unduly influenced by outside forces. When used as a legal term, informed consent is more clear-cut and enforce-able, but also much more limited. This chapter is concerned with exploring informed consent as an ethical ideal and looking at the way this ideal is realized for patients in Ireland today.

Informed Consent: The Ideal

In one of the leading texts on medical ethics, the ideal of informed consent is described as follows:

> A person gives an informed consent . . . if and only if the person, with substantial understanding and in substantial absence of control by others, intentionally authorises a healthcare professional to do something.[3]

This is the ideal adopted in this pamphlet and it is against this ideal that the reality of informed consent and its legal treatment will be measured. Understanding this ideal requires a closer look at the important concepts of 'substantial understanding' and 'in substantial absence of control by others'.

Substantial Understanding

The ideal of informed consent requires that the patient substan-tially understands the nature of the procedure he is authorizing. But, as ethicists Faden and Beauchamp point out[4], it also requires the patient to understand that *he* is authorizing the procedure; in other words, that he has a choice about whether the procedure will take place. Research carried out in the United States on the question of whether patients actually believe that they are authorizing a procedure indicates that a sizeable number of patients believe that they are simply being told what is happening and have no control over this.[5] Surveys of medical professionals have also suggested that a substantial number of doctors regard informed consent as involving information disclosure and treatment recommendation rather than permission or consent to treat.[6] Without this fundamental understanding on the part of both doctor and patient that the patient is the ultimate decision-maker, the provision of all the information in the world cannot give rise to informed consent.

Once the nature of the consent is understood, the patient must also understand the nature of his condition and of the treatment or procedure proposed. The way in which we view understanding in this context has important implications for the achievability of informed consent. If the standard of understanding is set too high (everything about the procedure, the risks, possibilities, limitations, all other options, and how each of these will impact on the patient as an individual), informed consent simply becomes impossible, not only because of the inevitable human frailties of both the patient and the doctor, but also because of scientific uncertainty. Sometimes, there simply are no straight answers. It is because of this that, even as an ideal, informed consent does not require full understanding but rather requires 'substantial understanding' which focuses on understanding the '*material* or *important* descriptions' in relation to a process.[7]

Achieving Substantial Understanding

The provision of information is an essential first step to the achievement of substantial understanding. In the vast majority of cases, a patient will not, at the outset, have sufficient information about the procedure or treatment for which his consent is sought and will be reliant on his doctor to inform him. Indeed, such is the importance of information that many patients and doctors mistakenly view the disclosure of information of itself to constitute informed consent.[8] From an ethical (rather than legal) perspective, the aim of disclosure is to achieve understanding on the part of the patient rather than to provide legal protection for the doctor. Thus, the manner in which information is communicated cannot be separated from the information itself.

Given the limited human capacity to take in information, massive information overload is as likely to cause confusion and impair understanding as the provision of inadequate information. Therefore, the ideal of informed consent does not require that all imaginable information be conveyed. Instead, ethicists use a two-level standard to determine how much information should be given. First are the 'core' disclosures. This is the information which patients or research subjects *usually* consider material (or worth considering) in deciding whether to consent and also the information that the medical professional believes to be material about the proposed intervention or research.[9] Unlike in legal discourse relating to information disclosure, there is no reference to the 'reasonable' patient or professional. Instead, the focus is on what patients usually consider to be important rather than on whether a patient is reasonable in doing so. It is also not necessary (again unlike the legal position) that there be a causal connection between the information provided and the decision made. Most patients will probably, in fact, discount much of the information they receive as irrelevant to the decision in hand.

Core disclosures would relate to matters such as the risks inherent in the procedure (more or less the sole legal test for disclosure); the success rates for the treatment and what those success rates mean; the benefits and side effects of the procedure as well as the uncertainties; the doctor's recommendation (in relation to medical procedures or therapeutic research); alternatives to the recommended procedure; the relative experience of the medical professional; the role of other members of a medical 'team' and the presence of students; and the costs and expenses of the procedure. These are the factors which patient surveys (mostly from the US and UK) indicate again and again are important to patients.[10] In the context of medical research, the category of 'core' disclosures would also include information about the purpose of the research; the bodies funding and organizing the research; and how the study will be carried out, including whether placebos will be used.

As the above list suggests, the category of 'core' disclosures is not fixed or immutable. It varies according to the procedure and the context. It requires medical professionals to be aware on an ongoing basis of the attitudes of their patients and of the society in which they live. In this regard, the shortage of specifically Irish surveys of patients in relation to information requirements is very unfortunate. It is very difficult for medical professionals to develop their skills in information disclosure (and indeed to take informed consent seriously) in the absence of culturally specific studies.

Within the standards of the ethical ideal, the category of 'core' disclosures is only the first step towards achieving substantial understanding. This goal can only be achieved on an individualized basis; just because most people would understand something does not mean that a specific individual has understood. It is on this basis that ethicists Faden and Beauchamp argue in favour of an additional level of information disclosure. This is the disclosure of information that 'is or would be viewed by *the actor* as worthy of consideration in the process of deciding about whether to perform a proposed action'.[11] This may seem like an impossibly high standard. How is the doctor to know what a particular patient will consider 'worthy of consideration'? The deceptively simple answer is that a doctor will only find out what information is relevant to the patient by listening to the patient. This focus on the individual patient regards communication of information as a two-way process. Achieving the ethical ideal of informed consent is therefore not just about imparting information but also about listening to the patient. Thus, discussion and clear (and sincere) statements about the medical professional's willingness to participate in discussion are as fundamental to the achievement of informed consent as information disclosure.

In the Absence of Control By Others

The second requirement for informed consent is that the decision should be made by the patient in the absence of control by others. This does not mean that other people should not be involved. Few people make important decisions completely unaided. As well as medical experts, family, friends, religious or other advisors are frequently relied on as sounding boards or for advice. This in no way runs counter to the ethical ideal of informed consent. Yet, as the following example taken from Schneider's book *The Practice of Autonomy* shows, sometimes the proponents of autonomy can get carried away in their enthusiasm to prevent outside influences on the patient. The practice of one burns unit in relation to relatives is described thus:

> When diagnosis is confirmed, the physician and other team members enter the room. Family members are not invited into the room to ensure that the decision of the patient is specifically his own.'[12]

It does not take much imagination to envisage what this must feel like for the patient. Traumatized and in pain, he finds his support structures withdrawn just when he has to make one of the most important decisions of his life. If this is the price of autonomy, then for many patients, the price is too high. Unless we view autonomy as requiring complete independence, there is no reason why other people, family, friends and others, should not play a role in the patient's deliberations. However, it is important that it is the patient and not any other interested party who sets the boundaries for who should be involved and how much that involvement should be.

Involving Others: The Importance of Confidentiality

While consent is a relative newcomer to ethical debate on medical matters, the duty of confidentiality may be traced to the Hipprocratic Oath where physicians promised:

> What I may see or hear in the course of treatment or even outside of the treatment in regard to the life of

> men, which on no account [ought to be] spread abroad,
> I will keep to myself, holding such things shameful to be
> spoken about.[13]

In its *Guide to Ethical Conduct and Behaviour*[14] the Irish Medical Council affirms the importance of confidentiality, noting that '[w]hile the concern of relatives and close friends is understandable, the doctor must **not** disclose information to any person without the consent of the patient' (original emphasis). This duty of confidence is also inherent in the individual's right to privacy guaranteed by Article 40.3.1 of the Irish Constitution and Article 8 of the European Convention on Human Rights and Fundamental Freedoms.

Achieving the balance between a respect for confidentiality and an acknowledgement of the importance of other people in most patients' lives is not always a simple matter. Surveys indicate that the vast majority of patients are happy to have information about their medical conditions given to their families, but, in almost all cases, with the proviso that their consent be sought first. Patients want their relatives to receive information partly for their relatives' benefit and also partly for their own. As one person in a survey of cancer patients noted:

> If your close family know, you can talk about it, which
> makes things easier than if you've just got to bottle
> everything up and are too frightened to . . . say some-
> thing in case you're going to upset somebody if they
> don't know.[15]

In the confusion of serious illness, it can sometimes be forgotten that, while only the patient may permit consultation with other interested parties, many patients will not be aware of this. As a result, the patient may not be consulted about how much information should be given to family and friends. Thus, there are times when the patient's confidence is respected at the expense of his welfare. This is reflected in the *National Patients Perception of the Quality of Healthcare Survey 2000*,[16] where the main complaint of

Irish patients in this regard was that their family and friends did not receive enough information. Almost one in ten patients surveyed held this view while only one in 500 patients felt that their families had received too much information.

Advice without Control: The Role of the Medical Professional

The requirement that a patient make his decision free from control raises questions about the role of the medical professional. Some medical professionals have adopted the view that autonomy means independence and have chosen to opt out of the patient's decision-making processes, in order to ensure that they do not unduly influence the patient. The resulting feelings of confusion, even betrayal, for many patients are evident in the following commentary by an English patient:

> When he asked me what I wanted him to do I was very upset. I mean he's meant to be the expert isn't he? How could I be expected to know what's the best if he doesn't? I thought it was cruel, I didn't know what to say. I asked him what he would do if it was his wife's X-ray and tests in front of him and he just said that what mattered was what I wanted. I don't think it's fair to say that to people like me who don't know much about illness and operations.[17]

For other practitioners, this kind of opting out is not an option. Informed consent does not remove a doctor's obligation to care for his patient. Thus, Professor David Jenkins (former Dean of Medicine at University College, Cork) argues that:

> What matters is that the patient consents to that course of action which best serves her total interests. If that course of action is clear to the doctor then his/her duty is to get her to consent to it.[18]

There is no difficulty with using reason and argument to persuade a patient to consent to a course of treatment. Thus, arguments such as 'this treatment has a good success rate' or 'there are comparatively few side effects with this treatment' or even 'if I were in your situation, I would probably go ahead with the treatment' (provided that this is true) would not constitute inappropriate control.

The more difficult task is to draw the line between advice and control, or, to adopt Jenkins' language, how much pressure can a doctor put on a patient in order to 'get her to consent'? Some forms of pressure are inherently incompatible with the ideal of informed consent. Coercion (using a credible threat in order to induce agreement) can never be compatible with informed consent. Thus, the doctor who says 'If you don't agree to this procedure, I will cease to treat you/tell your parents/report you to the authorities' cannot be said to have obtained his patient's informed consent. This does not mean that a doctor cannot point out the likely outcome of a proposed course of action ('If you do not agree to this treatment, you will die') so long as he is accurately representing an outcome that he does not control.

Obtaining a patient's consent through manipulation is also, by and large, incompatible with informed consent. Manipulation, in this context, may relate to the options made available to a patient where certain options are made more or less attractive depending on the desired behaviour. An example of this would be payment for blood transfusions or the early release for prisoners who participate in research trials. It may also relate to the information provided or the way in which information is given. An example would be the provision of information about risks only after the patient has psychologically committed to the procedure.[19]

The boundaries, especially those between persuasion and manipulation, are not always clear. How far can a medical professional go in pressuring a patient before the persuasion becomes coercion? How much latitude does a medical professional have in choosing how to represent an option before persuasion becomes manipulation?

There are no neat answers to the dilemma of how to persuade without taking control. Each situation needs a judgement that can only be made if the professional has experience, knowledge of the situation and of the patient and, most crucially, an inherent respect for the patient's right to make his own decision.

Informed Consent: The Reality

Professional Commitment to the Ideal

The *Charter of Rights for Hospital Patients* agreed by Irish hospitals in 1992 tells hospital patients that:

> Generally, treatment should only be given to a patient with his or her informed consent or in the case of a child, the consent of a parent or guardian. You may request the presence of a person or persons of your choosing during the procedure for granting consent. The consent form you are asked to sign should clearly state the nature of the procedure to be undertaken. Only in cases where a patient lacks the capacity to give or withhold consent, and where a qualified medical doctor determines that treatment is urgently necessary in order to prevent immediate or imminent harm, may treatment be given without informed consent.

Thus, patients are, in theory at least, made aware of the centrality of consent. The phrasing of the provision is unfortunate with the use of the word 'generally' at the beginning serving to rob the body of the provision of much of its rhetorical force. The *Charter* promises patients that their consent must be sought before their consultant can involve them in the teaching of students. Patients are also told that they have a right to information:

> You have a right to be informed of the nature of your illness or condition in language you can fully understand, and to be informed concerning:
> · Alternative forms of treatment
> · Results of tests/X-rays
> · The purpose, benefit and duration of planned treatment
> · Possible pain or discomfort, risks and side effects

This promise dovetails in part with one aspect of the ethical ideal of informed consent. It entitles patients to many of the core disclosures. However, it does not provide for the second individualized aspect of disclosure, in that it does not guarantee the patient that his specific informational needs will be met. In fact, amazingly, it does not even tell patients that they have a right to have their questions answered.

Although the *Charter* does provide for patient rights, it is limited in a number of crucial respects. First, it does not facilitate an exchange of information between doctor and patient but rather only the provision of information by the doctor. Secondly, it applies only to hospital patients. Thirdly, copies of the *Charter* are not widely available. It is not routinely issued to patients and is to be found on some noticeboards in some hospitals; outside of this, it is a surprisingly difficult document to access.[20] In these circumstances, it is difficult to see how patients can have any meaningful knowledge of their (relatively limited) rights under the *Charter*, let alone the wherewithal to enforce them.

Consent is referred to in the Medical Council's *Guide to Ethical Conduct and Behaviour* (1998).[21] However, it is not accorded a central position. In the introduction to the *Guide*, Professor Gerard Bury, the President of the Medical Council, describes patient welfare as being paramount. The word 'autonomy' and the term 'patients' rights' do not appear. A perusal of the *Guide* itself indicates that this is not an accident. Although the *Guide* is generally supportive of the notion of informed consent, it does not devote much space to setting out how this can be achieved. This is in part due to the 'catch-all' nature of the *Guide*, which covers matters ranging from how to set up and operate a practice and how to make locum arrangements, to more nebulous concepts such as responsibility and behaviour towards patients and professional responsibilities. The *Guide* contains a general provision relating to consent which provides that 'people have the right to refuse treatment or investigation'. Although there is no explicit mention of the refusal of life-saving treatment, one can assume that such refusal is included.[22] The doctor is told that he may assume tacit consent to investigations and procedures whenever consulted by a patient. This provision does go on to state that the doctor should make every effort to ensure that the patient understands the nature and purpose of the procedure proposed. Nonetheless, the weighting of the provision is in favour of a presumption of consent.

Although information and consent are inextricably linked, the *Guide* deals with the two questions separately. Under the heading 'Behaviour Towards Patients', doctors are told that they must always provide a positive response to a request for information from patients. Patients should be encouraged to ask questions and should be answered carefully in non-technical terms. This focus on achieving understanding rather than merely imparting information is a welcome inclusion. Unfortunately, however, the stated aim of the communication is 'to encourage compliance with recommended therapy'. Communication is clearly seen as a one-way street. There is no suggestion that doctors have an ethical obligation to listen to their patients' views (rather than their questions). There is no encouragement to facilitate patients in weighing up alternatives and to acknowledge the inevitable uncertainties of any course of treatment. The message is simply to find the recommended therapy and get the patient's agreement.

This rather paternalistic attitude may also be seen in the *Guide*'s treatment of access to medical records. While acknowledging that 'there is no objection to patients being supplied with a report of their own medical history', there is no positive encouragement to doctors to provide such reports. Thus, from the consent perspective, one might describe the *Guide* as recognizing in general terms the importance of consent and clear information but as still containing some paternalistic presumptions. Although the doctor should improve his communication skills and ensure understanding, ultimately, the *Guide* suggests, decisions are those of the doctor to which the patient should accede.

Informed Consent: Patients' Experiences

For many patients, the reality of consent which they experience is far removed from the ethical ideal set out above and indeed from the promises made in the *Charter of Rights for Hospital Patients* and the standards imposed by the Medical Council's *Guide to Ethical Conduct*. For these patients, the process of obtaining informed consent involves nothing more than appending their signature to a form. The form is frequently either framed in inaccessible language with complex medical terms setting out risks without adequate explanation, or it is so bland as to be effectively meaningless.[23] Often, too, the function of explaining the procedure and having the consent form signed is regarded as an unimportant detail, assigned to a younger member of a surgical team. Thus, in evidence to the Bristol Inquiry,[24] one doctor described how, as part of his training, he was sent, not to explain or to inform but 'to consent' patients.[25] Added to this is the fact that, in surgical situations, the question of consent is frequently broached for the first (and only) time very close to the time of the surgery, a time when patients are often frightened and disconcerted by the situation in which they find themselves. As such, they are not in the best position to take in information, especially information about risks. The result is that, in survey after survey relating to informed consent, patients have indicated that they do not understand the consent form they are signing and that they quickly forget even the most basic information relating to the procedures.[26]

That this is a large part of Irish patients' experience is reflected in the recent *National Patients Perception of the Quality of Health-care Survey 2000*.[27] This survey, which examines a range of issues relating to hospital treatment, is based upon 1,950 patients across 13 Irish hospitals. It is evident from the survey that informed consent remains an unattained ideal for many patients. Up to 15 per cent of respondents either could not understand information given by their doctors or nurses or were not offered information,[28] while 17.4 per cent of those undergoing tests during their hospital stay had received little or no explanation of the purpose of the test.[29] One in ten patients who were undergoing surgery during their hospital stay had not received any explanation of the surgical procedure planned.[30] Patient statements such as 'I would have liked the surgeon to discuss the operation beforehand' or 'I was nervous about the operation and would have liked to discuss it beforehand' indicate just how far some practices are from the ethical ideal. Furthermore, in spite of the promise in the *Charter of Rights for Hospital Patients* that a patient's permission must be sought before a consultant can involve him in teaching students, 42.2 per cent of patients visited by students stated that they had not had their permission requested prior to the visit.

The survey also indicated that patients were reluctant to seek further information. Almost one fifth of patients had questions that they would have liked to have asked their doctors but did not. A smaller number (13.4 per cent) of patients had questions that they would have liked to have asked their nurses. The reasons cited by patients for not asking their questions that either that staff were not around or were too busy, that staff did not like to be questioned, or that patients did not want to bother staff. Thus, patients' responses included 'I did not ask questions because I felt intimidated. There were too many doctors present and when I did ask questions I was given short replies' and 'I felt uncomfortable about asking questions. Doctors and nurses spoke about me the whole time as though I was not there.'

The findings in this Irish survey are replicated in surveys from other countries. In the UK *National Survey of Hospital Patients 1994*[31], 16 per cent of patients had been given no explanation of their condition or treatment. Almost one in five patients had no explanation of what would be done during surgery and 28 per cent had no discussion with staff about the risks and benefits of surgery. In an almost exact replication of the Irish findings, 42 per cent of patients were not asked for their prior permission for students to be present. Extensive (and more specific) surveys from the US yield similar findings.[32] The conclusion is that, even at the basic level of information disclosure, informed consent is not being consistently delivered.

4. Delivering Consent: The Role of Law

Many of the principles underlying the doctrine of informed consent find expression in legal discourse. It is indisputable that the law has played an important role in the popularization of informed consent and has been a means, in some cases the sole means, of ensuring some level of patient participation in their healthcare decisions. However, although the legal understanding of informed consent owes something to the ethical ideal of informed consent, the vision enshrined in the law is a much impoverished vision. This chapter explores the role of law in delivering informed consent and evaluates its contribution in this regard. In order to do this, a distinction must be made between the legal treatment of consent to research and consent to straightforward medical treatment. The crucial difference between the two areas is that consent to research is governed by legislation while, in most cases, consent to medical treatment operates outside of a legislative framework.

Consent to Research

In Ireland, research on human subjects is governed by the Control of Clinical Trials Act 1987 as amended by the Control of Clinical Trials and Drugs Act 1990. However, the passage of a recent European Directive relating to clinical trials[1] means that the Government will have to amend the existing position. As will be seen below, even without the need to comply with European law, the Irish legislation is in serious need of reform.

The impetus for the introduction of the 1987 Act was the public concern arising from the death of a young participant in a controlled trial in 1984. The man in question, who had been paid for participating in the trial, had not revealed to the investigating physician that he had been using certain drugs, which reacted with the drugs administered as part of the trial. In response to a public outcry, the Minister for Health introduced the legislation.

Under the legislation, anyone who intends to carry out a

clinical trial must obtain the permission of the Minister for Health and Children. This permission will only be forthcoming if an ethics committee (the membership of which has been approved by the Minister) has approved the trial.

The Act sets out some of the criteria to be considered by the ethics committee in deciding whether to grant the permission. These include the objectives of the trial, the qualifications of the parties involved and the risks to the proposed participants. An essential prerequisite for approval is that all participants have given written consent to their participation in the trial. These participants must be competent to understand the nature, significance and scope of their consent. The term 'informed consent' is not used. However, the Act does specify information which must be disclosed to the participants. This goes some way towards giving practical effect to the disclosure aspect of informed consent. Thus, the Act provides that the participant must be 'made aware' of matters such as the objectives of the trial; the manner in which the substance or preparation on trial is to be administered; the risks and any discomforts involved in the trial and the possible side effects of the trial; as well as whether or not a placebo will be administered to some persons.[2] Consent may be withdrawn at any time and there must be a six-day 'cooling-off' period between the provision of information and the commencement of the trial.[3] No inducement or reward may be offered in return for participation in the trial unless this has been specifically provided for in the permission.

If the clinical trial is of potential therapeutic benefit to the participant, some derogation from the consent requirement is permitted. A participant who is capable of understanding but physically incapable of giving consent in writing may give consent 'in any other manner' to a registered medical practitioner who is treating the patient for the illness covered by the trial.[4] If the participant is incapable of comprehending the nature, scope and significance of the consent given (for example, if she is a minor or a mentally incapacitated adult), a proxy may give written consent on her behalf if the proxy has been approved by the ethics committee and is independent of the applicant for permission.[5]

Like many pieces of reactive legislation, the Control of Clinical Trials Act 1987 is flawed in a number of respects. The consent section makes the mistake of focusing solely on information disclosure, and relatively limited disclosure at that. There is no statutory mention[6] of a requirement to provide information about who is funding the trial or, where the treatment may have therapeutic benefits, to provide alternatives to the treatment proposed. There is also no reference to achieving participant understanding. While it would be almost impossible for the law to require applicants to guarantee participant understanding, a requirement that applicants make all reasonable attempts to make the information accessible to their participants (and record these attempts in their application for permission) should be a basic part of the legislation. In this context also, although the Act provides that no reward or inducement to participate may be offered unless this has been specifically provided for in the permission, there is no provision in relation to threats or pressure to participate.[7]

The provisions dealing with proxy consent are also inadequate. Remarkably, there is no stated provision that participation in the trial must be in the *best* interests of the participant. Instead, the Act looks at the purpose for which the treatment is to be administered (i.e. that it is therapeutic) rather than at its likely effect on the patient. It is also extremely unsatisfactory in that there is no obligation to provide such information to the participant as she is able to understand. Even if an individual is incapable of giving consent, she may well be able to understand some aspects of the proposed trial if the procedure is explained in an accessible way.

It is undoubtedly true that an astute and careful ethics committee could make up for many of the deficiencies in the legislation by imposing conditions in its grant of permission for the trial. Nonetheless, as a legislative standard, the Act can still only be described as utterly inadequate. The European Directive on clinical trials referred to earlier must be introduced into national law by 1 May 2003. This Directive requires that a trial subject have 'had the opportunity, in a prior interview with the investigator or a member of the investigating team, *to understand* (author's emphasis) the objectives, risks and inconveniences of the trial . . .' Thus, mere disclosure will no longer be sufficient. The Directive also requires that minors and mentally incapacitated adults be given information about the trial and that, if an individual without the legal capacity to consent is capable of forming an opinion, her explicit wish to refuse participation in the trial or to withdraw from the trial must be considered by the principal investigator. The implementation of the Directive should therefore result in a much-needed, complete overhaul of the Control of Clinical Trials Act 1987 on the question of consent.

Consent to Medical Treatment

Other than the limited application of the Mental Health Act 2001 (which will be examined in Chapter 7), there are no legislative provisions relating to consent to medical treatment. The task of delivering informed consent is therefore left to the Constitution and to the law of tort.

Consent and the Constitution

The requirement for consent is the practical manifestation of the individual's rights to autonomy or self-determination and to bodily integrity. These rights are protected by the Irish Constitution.[8] In contrast to the fairly extensive discussions of rights in the context of proxy consent (discussed further in Chapter 7), there has been almost no judicial discussion of the role of the Constitution in protecting individual rights in the context of the personal right to consent.

There is one vague allusion to the constitutional right to bodily integrity in one of the leading tort cases in this area, *Walsh* v *Family Planning Service* (1992). This case concerned a man who had suffered considerable and most unpleasant complications following a vasectomy (to which he had consented). The High Court found that there was no negligence in the way in which the operation had been performed; however, the judge awarded the sum of £43,500 (€55,234) to the man on the basis that 'his constitutional right, that is an unspecified right to bodily integrity, has been violated'.[9] This award was overturned by the Supreme Court which dealt with the case on the more traditional basis of the law of tort. However, one judge, Justice McCarthy, did suggest that the Constitution might have some relevance to these kinds of cases but that the constitutional guarantee 'was not to be used to elevate a trifling cause of action'[10] (which he clearly believed would be the case here). The protection offered by the Constitution in this context therefore as yet remains more theoretical than real.

Delivering Informed Consent Through the Law of Tort

From a legal perspective the main task of delivering informed consent falls to the law of tort because of the absence of legislation and the fairly uninspiring constitutional record. The law of tort is a basically a compensation based system. It compensates claimants after they have suffered a wrong rather than preventing the wrong from occurring. This does not mean that the law of tort cannot influence future behaviour; if a person knows that she will have to pay compensation if she behaves in a particular way, she is likely to change her behaviour, if for no reason other than to avoid being sued.

As seen in Chapter 1, the earliest cases based on medical interventions in the absence of consent were taken in the tort of battery. The claimant's argument was the simple one that she had been subjected to physical contact to which she had not consented. Once the fact of the contact and the lack of consent had been established, the claimant did not have to show that she had suffered harm as a result. Her case was concluded regardless of the impact of the procedure on her. As the notion of consent became more sophisticated, more claimants began to argue that although, in strict terms, they had given consent to a procedure, this consent was not valid because they had not been given sufficient information about the procedure. In other words, their consent was not an informed consent. As informed consent claims became more commonplace, the question arose as to where this new action should be based. During this debate, it was persuasively argued by a leading commentator[11] that it was overly harsh on doctors to regard medical treatment without informed consent as battery. Battery, he argued, was symboli- cally associated in the public's mind with bad or immoral behaviour. Because doctors were acting in good faith and in the interests of their patients, it was not fair to categorize them in a way that suggested some kind of moral blameworthiness.

As a result of this argument, and beginning with the influen- tial US decision of *Canterbury* v *Spence* (1972), the legal responsibility for delivering informed consent shifted from the tort of battery to the tort of negligence. This view has been accepted by the courts in Ireland and in all the other common law countries.[12] This means that a claimant who argues that her consent to a medical procedure was not an informed one must make a case in the tort of negligence. As will be seen in the next section, this has had enormous consequences for the capacity of the law to deliver informed consent.

Establishing Negligence

In the typical negligence case based on the absence of informed consent, the claimant will have given consent to surgery. The surgery is carried out properly but through no fault of the doctor something goes wrong and the patient suffers harm as a result. In other words, a risk materializes. The claimant then argues that, when she gave her consent, she had not known about this risk and that, if she had known, she would not have had the surgery. Therefore, her consent was not an informed consent and her doctor is guilty of negligence for proceeding with the surgery in the absence of informed consent.

The leading Irish case of *Walsh* v *Family Planning Services* (1992) shows how this scenario can occur in practice. Here, the claimant consented to a vasectomy, which was carried out with all the necessary skill and care. However, unfortunately, he experienced a range of problems following the procedure. These problems included severe pain in the groin area (which was exacerbated during sexual intercourse), impotence and the eventual surgical removal of his left testicle (against medical advice). The claimant said that he had not been told about these risks when he gave his consent to the vasectomy. He argued that, if he had known about these risks at that time, he would not have consented to the procedure.

In order to succeed in a negligence action, a claimant had two tasks. The first is to show that her doctor should have provided her with certain information and that she did not do so. The second task is to show that if she had been provided with the information, she would not have had the surgery. Each task brings its own difficulties.

What Information Should be Provided?

Courts across the world have sought to develop a universal standard setting out in general terms what information should be provided to patients in order that their consent to surgery will be an informed one. This task has not been an easy one as is evidenced by the fact that, in spite of a number of important cases, the approach of the Irish courts is still not entirely clear.

In brief, two possible universal standards have been mooted. Both are concerned only with information about risks in a procedure. The first standard requires that physicians disclose all the risks in a procedure that a reasonable patient would want to know. This test has been adopted by the American, Australian and Canadian courts. The test is essentially patient-centred. In deciding how much information a patient should receive, the court places itself in the shoes of the patient and decides what a reasonable person *in the patient's position* would want to know. The way in which this standard works may be seen in the Australian case of *Rogers* v *Whittaker* (1992). In this case, the defendant eye surgeon had failed to tell the claimant that there was a very slight risk (1 in 14,000) that the proposed surgery to improve the sight in her, almost blind, right eye might lead to a loss of sight in her left eye. This risk materialized, leaving the plaintiff almost totally blind. Although the risk was very slight, the Court considered that the patient should have been told about it because she had made it very clear to the surgeon that she was most concerned about protecting her left eye.

This patient-centred approach has been rejected by the English courts which have preferred to ask what a reasonable doctor would consider appropriate to tell a patient[13] This test is two steps removed from the ethical ideal of informed consent. First, it focuses on doctors rather than patients and, secondly, it takes no account of the patient's individual position. This is reflected in the decision in *Blyth* v *Bloomsbury AHA* (1993) where the Court of Appeal held that, even though the patient had made specific inquiries (in this case, about the side effects of the injectible contraceptive, Depo-Provera), the doctor did not have an obligation to give the patient all the information that the reasonable patient would want to know. The question remains focused on the doctor and what she thinks is reasonable.

In the two leading Irish cases in this area, *Walsh* v *Family Planning Services* (1992) and *Bolton* v *Blackrock Clinic* (1997), the Supreme Court has leaned towards a standard based on what the reasonable doctor would have disclosed. In *Walsh*, one member of the Court (Chief Justice Finlay) specifically adopted the reasonable doctor standard in deciding how much informa-tion should have been given to a man prior to a vasectomy operation. In *Bolton*, Chief Justice Hamilton, with the agreement of the other two members of the Court, also adopted this stan-dard in deciding how much information should have been given to the patient prior to obtaining her consent to lung surgery. However, there is still some judicial support for the patient-centred test – in *Walsh*, one of the judges (Justice O'Flaherty) opted for this standard. This was also the accepted standard in the most recent decision in the area, that of Justice Kearns in the High Court in *Geoghegan* v *Harris* (2000). Justice Kearns' judg-ment is a thoughtful and coherent analysis of the question which ultimately concludes in favour of the reasonable patient test. Although a High Court decision, the quality of the judgment may lead to it having a broader acceptance than the rather empty Supreme Court judgment in *Bolton*.

The decision to adopt a patient-centred standard has undoubted symbolic importance. However, it would be a mistake to accord too much practical legal significance to the decision. After all, in most situations, the reasonable doctor will want to tell more or less what the reasonable patient will want to know. It is, in fact, the other aspect of the negligence action, namely the need to show harm, that poses the most difficulty for claimants.

The Need to Show Harm

Even if the claimant can show that the doctor should have given her more information, she will not necessarily succeed in her negligence action. This is because it is not enough for a claimant to show that the defendant behaved negligently; she must also show that she suffered harm *because of* the negligence. She must therefore show that, if the doctor has told her about the risk in the procedure, she would not have gone ahead with the procedure and so would have avoided the harm that befell her. The problem for claimants is that, because in the vast majority of cases the risks associated with a procedure are quite small and the potential benefits are quite large, most claimants cannot convincingly argue that they would have acted any differently even if they had been provided with a full picture.

This may be seen in *Geoghegan* v *Harris* (2000), where the claimant lost his legal action in spite of the judge's acceptance of a patient-centred test for disclosure. The claimant here had a bone graft from his chin to his jaw in order to enable dental implants to take place. The reasons for the procedure were essentially cosmetic. Unfortunately and through no fault of the doctor, in the process of the bone graft, the plaintiff suffered damage to his incisive nerve at the front of his chin leaving him with an ongoing condition of severe pain. The claimant argued that if he had known of the risk that this might happen, he would not have proceeded with the surgery. Justice Kearns asked what would a reasonable person *in the claimant's position* have done if he had been properly informed. Noting that the claimant had been very keen on having the surgery, Justice Kearns held that a reasonable person in his position would have gone ahead even if he had been informed of the risk, which was extremely remote. The claimant had therefore failed to show that his injury was caused by the failure to disclose and was prevented from recovering.

Disclosing Information Outside of Risks

Although the courts have been very active in promoting the provision of information to patients about risks, there has been much less discussion on the disclosure of other types of information. The result, noted by Jay Katz in his leading work, *The Silent World of Doctor and Patient*, has been that:

> Since the promulgation of the informed consent doctrine . . . physicians have of necessity become more aware of their new obligations to talk with patients about recommended treatments. Yet, by and large any disclosures have been limited to informing patients about the risks and benefits of proposed treatments, not about alternatives, and surely not about the certainties and uncertainties inherent in most treatment options.[14]

There are some signs that this legal position is changing, at least in North America. In one Canadian case,[15] the Saskatchewan Court of Appeal held a doctor liable for failing to tell a patient that there was an alternative, more conservative, treatment available than that advocated by the doctor. Other courts have required information to be given about the possible consequences of the patient's refusing treatment. Thus, in the Californian case of *Truman* v *Thomas* (1980), a doctor was held liable because he did not advise a patient of the consequences of her refusal to have a cervical smear when the patient subsequently died from cervical cancer.

There are also a number of decisions, again primarily from the United States, that suggest that the doctor must give the patient certain information about the doctor herself rather than just about the procedure. In *Perna* v *Pirozzi* (1983), the New Jersey Supreme Court held that a doctor was liable for failing to tell a patient that the surgical procedure to which the patient had consented might be performed by another surgeon. The claimant here believed that his surgery for the removal of kidney stones would be carried out by the defendant and he signed a consent form to this effect, but the surgery was in fact carried out by another (fully qualified) surgeon. The Court held that 'a patient has a right to know who will operate and the consent form should reflect the patient's decision'.

Along similar lines is the decision of the Maryland Court of Appeals that a surgeon had an obligation to inform patients that he was HIV positive[16] and the decision in the celebrated Californian case of *Moore* v *Regents of the University of California* (1990).[17] The claimant in this extraordinary case had an unusual cell line which was of great value commercially and scientifically. The defendant doctor and hospital used the claimant's spleen (which the doctor had removed because it was diseased) and various body products for research from which they intended to benefit financially and competitively. At no stage was the claimant told of his situation or of the research on his body parts. The Californian Supreme Court held that a doctor must tell a patient about 'personal interests unrelated to the patient's health, whether research or economic, that may affect his medical judgment'.

The American courts still resist the claim that a doctor should reveal the statistical prognosis for a patient's condition. In one Californian case,[18] the claimant's husband had pancreatic cancer, for which the statistical prognosis is that only about 5 per cent of patients survive for 5 years. The claimant unsuccessfully argued that if her husband had known that he would probably live only a short time, he would not have undergone painful experimental cancer treatment but rather would have chosen to live out his life in peace and put his business affairs in order. Also unknown to the patient in this case was the fact that the success of the treatment was determined on the basis of added months of survival rather than cure.

There has been almost no discussion in the Irish or English courts of the legal requirement to provide the patient with information regarding these important issues outside of risks.[19] There is no reason in principle why the Irish courts could not extend the negligence action to cover at least some of these situations. Such an extension would certainly widen the legal ambit of informed consent and bring this aspect of information disclosure closer to the ethical ideal.

Evaluating Law's Contribution

As patient surveys indicate, although consent to medical research and treatment is routinely required, the ethical ideal of informed consent has not been delivered. Yet, in spite of this and notwithstanding numerous attempts, there has never yet been a successful legal action before the Irish courts based on the absence of consent. The law of tort and especially the negligence action, which has become the focal point of the legal treatment of consent, is incapable of delivering informed consent. This is in part because judges have concentrated too much on the question of disclosure of risks and have failed to develop other aspects of the negligence action. Furthermore, although proper communication of information is clearly important in order to ensure that patients understand the information conveyed, there has been almost no judicial commentary on the question of the effectiveness of communication.[20] The result is that 'informed consent' for many patients and doctors consists of a rushed explanation or none at all, followed by a signature on a consent form listing risks. Informed consent as delivered by the law could hardly be further from the ethical ideal.

It is rather ironic that the law, which has substantially failed to deliver informed consent, has at the same time managed to antagonize many in the medical profession. Law is seen as a blunt instrument, incapable of taking into account the complexities of medical practice. Perhaps as a result, some members of the medical profession appear to regard informed consent as a legal nicety, to be complied with simply in order to keep the lawyers off their backs. In this way, consent becomes the consent form; disclosure a process to avoid being sued.

5. Competent to Consent?

A fundamental aspect of both the ethical ideal and the legal definition of informed consent is that the patient whose consent is at issue is capable of understanding the nature of the treatment or procedure proposed and of making a decision about whether to proceed. A patient who does not have this capacity cannot give consent and, other than in an emergency situation, a medical professional who proceeds to treat could be found liable in the tort of battery.

The ways in which decisions are made for two categories of patients who cannot give personal consent (children and adults without the necessary mental capacity) will be examined in Chapters 6 and 7. This chapter deals with a preliminary question, namely how it is decided whether or not a patient is competent to give consent. Ensuring that this decision is made properly is crucial from both an ethical and a legal perspective. If a patient is inappropriately deemed to be incompetent, his right to autonomy is significantly compromised and he loses the right to make decisions about his medical treatment. On the other hand, if a patient is inappropriately deemed to be competent, his consent is meaningless and his doctor is placed in a difficult legal position.

Before looking at the legal framework within which decisions about patients' competence are made, it is important to set out the underlying principles that must be acknowledged if these decisions are to be made in a way which recognizes the importance of patient autonomy.

Determining Competence and Maintaining Autonomy

If we are to take the principle of patient autonomy seriously, there are three basic principles that must be recognized in making decisions about whether a patient is competent. First, a decision relating to competence must always refer to a specific task. A person may not be categorized as generally incompetent but may only be deemed to be incompetent in relation to his ability to perform a particular task. This means that a patient may be competent to consent to some kinds of medical treatment while not being competent to consent to others. Thus, the law's traditional categorization of certain classes of people (children, mentally disabled or mentally ill people and, at one time, women) as automatically incapable of making certain types of decisions is inconsistent with this basic principle.

Secondly, a patient must be facilitated in reaching an understanding of the treatment proposed. It is not enough to provide a patient with information if this information is provided in a way that is inaccessible to him. Every effort must be made through sensitive use of language and the employment of other means of communication (tapes, videos, pictures, diagrams) to achieve patient understanding. Studies have shown that when simple steps to facilitate greater understanding were employed, patients who had previously been deemed incapable were found to have the necessary mental ability to direct their own healthcare decisions.[1] It is fundamental that every effort is made to ensure that patients are offered this opportunity.

The third principle is that there is no inherent connection between the rationality of a patient's decision and the patient's competence. Just because the medical professional, the court and indeed the vast majority of society would disagree with a decision, does not mean that the person making the decision is incompetent. The opposite view would make a mockery of a fundamental aspect of informed consent, namely the right to say no. It can at times be difficult to distinguish between a person who makes an irrational or unpopular decision and a person who is incompetent. While the fact that a person makes an irrational decision may sometimes indicate that the person is incompetent, it is also true that a decision that is irrational from one perspective may be entirely logical from another. Thus, in one English case (discussed below), a man refused to consent to a medically recommended below-the-knee amputation. However, as the judge discovered when he inquired further, the operation had a 15 per cent mortality rate. When viewed with this knowledge, the decision was not so irrational after all. The difficulties with deciding whether a person is competent are increased because the person charged with making an initial decision is often the person whose medical advice is being rejected. Even with the best intentions, it is very difficult for a medical professional to accept that a person who refuses to accept best advice and earnest entreaties can be competent. Yet this is what medical professionals are sometimes required to do.

Determining Competence: The Legal Frameworks

Determining Young People's Competence

Section 23 (1) of the Non-Fatal Offences Against the Person Act 1997 states that a person of more than 16 years can consent to 'surgical, medical or dental treatment' and that the consent of his parent or guardian is not necessary.[2] The section does not refer to refusal of treatment and it is unclear whether this is also implied. The section does not specifically prohibit young people aged less than 16 years from giving a legal consent to treatment and it remains to be seen whether the section will be interpreted as being facilitative (giving an automatic power to consent to young people aged more than 16 but not preventing all young people aged less than 16 years from giving a valid consent) or preventative (preventing all young people aged less than 16 from giving a valid consent). The first interpretation obviously shows a greater respect for young people's autonomy.

In the UK, where a provision similar to section 23 of the 1997 Act applies, the courts have held that a young person aged less than 16 years can give consent to treatment provided that he has 'sufficient maturity to understand what is involved'.[3] This means that, for any young person aged less than 16 years, there must be an individualized assessment of his competence. This assessment is to be undertaken by the medical professional who will provide the treatment. In the leading English case in this area, *Gillick* v *West Norfolk and Wisbech A.H.A* (1986), a majority of the House of Lords held that a mature young person may consent even to contraceptive treatment.[4] However, in a situation like this, the standard of maturity will be quite high. In the words of Lord Scarman:

> [T]here is much that has to be understood by a girl under the age of 16 if she is to have legal capacity to consent to such treatment. It is not enough that she should understand the nature of the advice which is being given: she must also have sufficient maturity to understand what is involved. There are moral and family questions, especially her relationship with her parents; long term problems associated with the emotional impact of pregnancy and its termination; and there are the risks to health of sexual intercourse at her age, risks which contraception may diminish but cannot eliminate.[5]

The English courts have had more difficulty in accepting that a young person aged between 16 and 18 years can refuse treatment, especially when this treatment is necessary to save the young person's life. The Court of Appeal has held that the refusal of life-saving treatment may be overridden either by the young person's parents or by the court (acting in his best interests).[6] Complete autonomy for young people is therefore limited and, in some life-and-death circumstances, must be balanced with a concern for the young person's welfare.

In Ireland, even if section 23 of the Non-Fatal Offences Against the Person Act 1997 is interpreted in a way that permits some young people below the age of 16 to give a valid consent, we still do not know how the Irish courts would respond to a situation similar to that in *Gillick* where contraceptive treatment was at issue. It is at least arguable that Article 42 of the Irish Constitution that guarantees the inalienable right and duty of parents to provide for the 'religious and moral, intellectual, physical and social education of their children' would prevent an interpretation of the 1997 Act that would interfere with a parental right to control their children's access to contraceptive treatment. The absence of clarity puts doctors in a very difficult position. How is a doctor to respond to a request by a 15-year-old girl to provide contraceptive treatment or the morning-after pill without the consent or knowledge of her parents? While each doctor's decision will depend on his view of the circumstances at hand, he is hampered in reaching this decision by the absence of clarity in relation to the legal framework that binds him.

Determining Mental Capacity

The recently introduced Mental Health Act 2001 provides that a patient's consent to treatment must be obtained provided that he is 'capable of understanding the nature, purpose and likely effects of the proposed treatment'. This judgement must be made by the consultant psychiatrist responsible for the care and treatment of the patient.[7] As will be seen in Chapter 7, this Act applies only to people suffering from a 'mental disorder' (defined narrowly) and to treatment 'intended for the purposes of amelio-rating a mental disorder'.[8] Outside of the context of the Act, there is no stated legal test for determining competence to consent. There is also little professional guidance for ordinary doctors[9] although Irish psychiatrists, who are members of the Royal Society of Psychiatrists based in London, are provided with guidelines on *Good Psychiatric Practice* (2000).[10] Although these guidelines have no legal effect in Ireland, they do provide an indication of the psychiatric profession's view of what is reasonable, a factor that would be likely to influence an Irish court.

The guidelines on *Good Psychiatric Practice* are based on a test laid down by the English High Court in *Re C (adult: refusal of medical treatment)* (1994). Under this test, a patient is competent to give consent to a procedure if he can:

(a) understand and retain the information relevant to the decision in question;
(b) believe that information; and
(c) weigh that information in the balance to arrive at a choice.

The test may be seen in operation in the case of *Re C* itself. This case concerned a 68-year-old man who suffered from chronic paranoid schizophrenia and who had been resident in a mental institution for almost 30 years. He developed a serious ulcer on his leg and expert medical opinion suggested that he would die if he did not have this leg amputated below the knee. C objected to the amputation, saying that he would rather die with two legs than live with one. When giving evidence, C was delusional, recollecting an international career in medicine in which he had never lost a patient and also imagining persecutions. However, he appeared to understand his medical situation. He accepted that death could be a consequence of his refusal to have the amputation, but repeated that he did not wish to have one. He was quite happy to co-operate with medical advice in all other respects. Using the three-part test set out above, Justice Thorpe held that, in spite of the fact that C's general capacity had been impaired by schizophrenia, in relation to the operation he had understood and retained the information given to him, believed it (in his own fashion) and reached a decision on the basis of it. His refusal to consent to the amputation was therefore allowed to stand.[11]

In the absence of any Irish discussion of the question, the test in *Re C* provides a useful reference point for medical professionals working in Ireland. The test has advantages over the test set down in the Mental Health Act 2001 because, as well as looking at the patient's capacity to understand the proposed treatment, it also looks at the patient's capacity to believe the information and to apply it to his individual situation.[12] It recognizes, for example, that a person suffering from a compulsive disorder such as anorexia nervosa might be entirely able to comprehend intellectually that death is the inevitable consequence of not eating, but he might not be able to accept that this information relates to his own situation.

Evaluating the Irish Legal Position

Two imperatives should govern the law's approach to decisions about a patient's competence. The first is the need to protect both the patient's autonomy and his welfare. The second is the need to give the medical professional some degree of guidance as regards how he should carry out this important function. The uncertainties in the Irish legal position do no favours to either the medical profession or the patient. The task of determining a patient's competence will always be a difficult one. Expecting medical professionals to carry out this task while wearing a legal blindfold is expecting too much.

6. Deciding For Children

There are few events more stressful that the serious illness of one's child. The American writer Lorrie Moore describes the moment of realization that a child is seriously ill:

> What words can be uttered? You turn just slightly and there it is: the death of your child. It is part symbol, part devil, and in your blind spot all along, until, if you are unlucky, it is completely upon you.[1]

Yet children do become ill and, when they do, someone has to make medical decisions for them. In most cases, this enormous responsibility falls on the child's parents who have both the legal right and the moral responsibility to decide whether to consent to medical treatment on behalf of their child.

Informed Parental Consent?

In most respects, parental consent is no different to personal consent and it certainly requires no less attention to the ethical ideal of informed consent. Thus, the ideal of informed parental consent is achieved where a parent or parents 'with substantial understanding and in substantial absence of control by others, intentionally authorises a healthcare professional to do something [to their child]'.[2] However, there are important differences between personal autonomy and parental autonomy. First, parents do not have an absolute right to refuse medical treatment on behalf of their child. Secondly, it is legitimate in some circumstances to second-guess parents' views of what constitutes their child's welfare. This does not mean that parents' views are not important and that their contribution, as the people who (in most cases) know the child best and care most about the child's welfare, should not be accorded the greatest weight. The challenge, therefore, is to respect parental autonomy without losing sight of the fact that, in some circumstances, there can be a conflict between parental autonomy and the welfare of the child. The response of the Irish courts to this challenge will be examined below.

The Limits of Parental Autonomy

The Irish Constitution dictates, in large part, the extent to which Irish parents are free to make decisions about their children's health. The Constitution bestows considerable rights on 'the Family' in Article 41 and on 'the Family' and on 'parents' in Article 42.[3] Article 41.1 states that:

> The State recognizes the Family as the natural primary and fundamental unit group of Society, and as a moral institution possessing inalienable and imprescriptible rights, antecedent and superior to all positive law.

Article 42 states that the 'primary and natural educator of the child is the Family' and provides in Article 42.5 that the State may 'supply the place of the parents' only in *exceptional* cases where the parents 'for physical or moral reasons fail in their duty towards their children'.

Within this framework, some limitations on parental autonomy are widely accepted and are relatively uncontroversial. Thus, for example, parental autonomy would not permit the refusal of treatment on religious grounds where the treatment in question is necessary to save their child's life. This may be seen in a case heard before the Waterford District Court where the parents of a young boy refused on religious grounds (they were Jehovah's Witnesses) to consent to a blood transfusion for the child.[4] The child was taken into care under section 12 of the Child Care Act 1991,[5] and an emergency order of the District Court was issued permitting the transfusion to go ahead. The decision was not a difficult one; the child's right to life clearly took precedence over the parents' rights. The parents in question indicated that they were happy to abide by the court's views and the child was returned to his parents' care within 72 hours. Other cases are more difficult. How much latitude, for example, do parents have in refusing life-saving treatment for a child (who may perhaps have already undergone extensive surgery and chemotherapy) because they believe that their child should not suffer any more?[6]

Outside of life-and-death questions, the Irish courts have indicated that parents do possess substantial autonomy in relation to their children's healthcare decisions. In *North Western Health Board* v *HW and CW* (2000), the parents of a new-born baby refused to consent to the carrying out of the PKU test (commonly known as the 'heel test') on their child. The PKU test is a relatively minor test, which enables certain metabolic conditions to be diagnosed at an early stage while they may still be easily treated. Refusal of the test is rare but an average of six or seven sets of parents annually do refuse their consent to the test. In this case, the parents' refusal was based on a range of reasons, unconnected to religious beliefs, which focused on the fact that the test involved puncturing a blood vessel. In the High

Court, Justice McCracken declined to override the parents' refusal, arguing that their behaviour in refusing to consent did not come within the 'exceptional cases' referred to in Article 42.5 of the Constitution which entitles the State to interfere with parental rights. In the judge's words:

> If the State were entitled to intervene in every case where professional opinion differed from that of the parents, or where the State considered the parents were wrong in a decision, we would be rapidly stepping into the Brave New World in which the State always knows best.[7]

Justice McCracken's decision was upheld by the Supreme Court, where the Court accepted that the effect of denying the parents the right to refuse in this case would be to make the PKU test compulsory in Ireland without any legislative decision in this regard. The Court noted that the test was not compulsory in any other European country or in the United States. The decision about whether to consent to the test was regarded as being no different to the many decisions relating to their children's welfare made by parents.[8] In the words of Justice Denham:

> Every day, all over the State, parents make decisions relating to the welfare, including physical, of their children. Having received information and advice they make a decision. It may not be the decision advised by the doctor (or teacher, or social worker, or psychologist, or priest or other expert) but it is the decision made, usually responsibly, by parents and is abided by as being in the child's best interest. Having been given the information and advice, responsibility remains with parents to make a decision for their child. The parents are responsible and liability rests with them as to the child's welfare.

The recognition given to parental autonomy under the Irish Constitution does not necessarily prevent any interference outside the obvious life-and-death situations. As the Supreme

Court acknowledged in the *North Western Health Board* case, each case requires the importance of parental autonomy to be balanced against the child's welfare (ultimately as determined by a court) in the circumstances at hand. Thus, as the consequences of parental refusal become more serious or the grounds for the parents' objections become less serious, the justification for interference with parental autonomy grows. When the threat to the child's welfare becomes too great, it is both ethically desirable and legally justifiable to interfere.

Informing Parental Consent

Many of the realities surrounding parental consent to children's surgery came to public attention during the Public Inquiry Into Children's Heart Surgery at the Bristol Royal Infirmary 1984–1995. In July 2001, Professor Ian Kennedy, Chair of the Inquiry, presented the Report of the Inquiry, aptly entitled *Learning from Bristol.*[9] Concluding that up to one-third of the children treated by the clinic had received inadequate care, leading to the unnecessary death of up to 35 babies under the age of one, the report summarizes its findings as follows:

> The story of the paediatric cardiac surgical service in Bristol is not an account of bad people. Nor is it an account of people who did not care, nor of people who wilfully harmed patients... It is an account of a hospital where there was a club culture, an imbalance of power, with too much control in the hands of a few individuals. It is an account in which vulnerable children were not a priority, either in Bristol or throughout the NHS.[10]

As part of its investigation, the Inquiry looked at consent and communication practices as they operated at the clinic. Clinic practices in both regards were found to be seriously deficient. Some parents had not been told that they had a choice about where to take their child for surgery, other parents felt that they had not been given an accurate picture of risks and survival rates. The Inquiry also found that the cardiologists had, sometimes deliberately, painted too optimistic a picture for parents. One cardiologist expressed the view that his duty was to try to maintain hope.[11] While this is understandable, it placed parents in a false position, adding to their later distress and undermining their trust in their children's medical team. One parent, in her evidence to the Inquiry, spoke about why honesty was so important, especially when a child is very sick:

> I think you need to know. It hurts . . . It hurts to hear it, but you need to know the truth. I do not want to be told that everything is going to be jolly and fine. It is a fact of life . . . You do not want people to be cruel to you but you need honesty in a situation like that.[12]

On the important question of communication of information, the Inquiry found that while some parents had received thorough explanations of the surgery proposed, others testified that they had received a hurried account assisted only by drawings on scraps of paper and even on paper towels.[13] The Inquiry concluded that there was a sense that the process of obtaining consent was something of a chore, ideally to be delegated to junior staff.

As recognized at the Bristol Inquiry, parents should be recognized and treated as partners with medical professionals in the task of making decisions about their children.[14] Thus, the importance of attaining the ideal of informed consent is, if anything, even more important in the context of parental consent. Yet, the difficulty of attaining informed consent is increased in the stressful climate created by a child's illness. Not only are the parents under enormous personal pressures, they also have to make a fundamentally important decision on behalf of another person and will have to live with the consequences of this decision for the rest of their lives. The inadequacy of the legal understanding of informed consent is nowhere more apparent than in relation to informed parental consent. It is futile (unless the aim is simply to avoid legal actions) to go through the motions of reciting risks to stressed and emotional parents and obtaining their signatures to consent forms. A great deal more effort at communication is needed if parental consent is to be meaningful.

In the focus on informed parental consent, it is important not to forget that the child herself must also be consulted. Even if a child is not legally competent to give consent for herself, she should still be kept informed of her treatment in a language and manner that she can understand. In addition, her views should be sought and, where possible, respected as a matter of course.[15]

7. Deciding for Adults

Adults and children with mental illness and intellectual disability, and elderly people suffering from dementia, have been among the most abused members of society, not just in Ireland but throughout the world. Frequently vulnerable and unable to protect their own interests, these groups of people have suffered economically, socially, and educationally, as well as medically. The classic film, *One Flew Over the Cuckoo's Nest*,[1] made accessible to a wider audience some of the abuses endured by mentally vulnerable people in an uncaring society. Few people who saw the film will forget the brutal way in which the nonconformist patient, McMurphy (played by Jack Nicholson) was finally silenced.

Consenting for Adults: Whose Decision?

No One to Consent

Under Irish law, once a person reaches the age of eighteen[2] there is nobody with the legal capacity to give a proxy consent to medical treatment on his behalf. This is the case even if, because of mental illness or intellectual disability, a person is incapable of giving personal consent. It is also the case where a patient is temporarily unconscious and unable to consent on his own behalf. This legal gap does not mean that all medical treatment is unlawful. Treatment that is medically necessary in an emergency situation will be lawful and the medical professional will have a defence to any charge of battery.[3]

Outside of emergency situations, there is a limited, and woefully inadequate, facility to enable consent to be given on behalf of an adult who lacks mental capacity. This arises under the outdated Lunacy Regulations (Ireland) Act, 1871, whereby an adult who has been determined to be an 'idiot, lunatic, or of unsound mind, and incapable of managing himself or his affairs' may be made a ward of court. When this happens, a wardship committee (normally a single person, in spite of the name) who is usually a close relative of the ward is appointed to take control of the ward's affairs. The wardship committee may give proxy consent to medical treatment in some circumstances. However, court permission is required for serious procedures. The primary difficulty with the wardship facility is that the procedure is complex, expensive and cumbersome. This means that wardship applications are really only made in practice where the management of property is involved. As a result, most legally incompetent adults have no legally recognized representative to act on their behalf.

For people who are not wards of court and for wards of court whose treatment is sufficiently serious, the final legal authority to consent to medical treatment is located in the High Court. The Court's power in this regard originates from the power of the King in feudal times to make decisions for those of his subjects who were incapable of taking control of their own affairs. In time, this power, known as the *parens patriae* (or 'parent of the country') jurisdiction, was passed to the courts.[4] In making its decision, the court must act in the best interests of the individual involved.

The only reported Irish example of the use of the *parens patriae* jurisdiction in relation to medical treatment arose in *In Re a Ward of Court* (1995). In this case, the family of the ward wished to end life-sustaining treatment (in this case hydration and nutrition), which had kept the ward alive in a near-PVS for the previous 23 years. Because of the serious nature of the proposed intervention, the family applied to the High Court for its permission to end the treatment. In the High Court and, on appeal in the Supreme Court, permission to end the treatment was granted. The Court held that the test to be applied was whether, from the perspective of a prudent, good and loving parent, the proposed treatment was in the best interests of the individual involved. In this case, it was held to be in the ward's best interests that her life should not be prolonged any more.

Making Decisions in Practice

The lack of a proper legal structure does not mean that medical decisions are not all the time being made on behalf of people who cannot give personal consent. Medical professionals, working with families and carers, must reach decisions about the treatment to be given or when treatment should be with-drawn. This is reflected in the Medical Council's *Guide to Ethical Conduct and Behaviour* (1998), which advises doctors to consult with parents, guardians and relatives.[5] This consultative process has advantages. It involves the people who know the patient best and who, in most cases, have the patient's best interests at heart in a manner which is simple, cheap and non-confrontational. From the doctor's perspective, it also reduces the risk of legal actions; if the interested parties have been consulted, they are less likely to sue.

However, this process of decision-making has no legal basis. We simply do not know the circumstances in which an Irish court would permit medical treatment of a patient who cannot give a personal consent. Faced with a similar difficulty, the English courts have held that a doctor who treats a patient without consent is not acting unlawfully provided that the treat-ment in question is in the best interests of the patient as determined by the doctor.[6] Deciding best interests, in this context, requires an evaluation of emotional and welfare inter-ests as well as medical ones.[7] In the event of a dispute as to what constitutes the patient's best interests, the court will be the ultimate arbiter. The English courts have also held that certain types of medical intervention are so serious that they require prior court approval. These situations include sterilization for contraceptive purposes; the donation of human tissue or organs; and the withdrawal of hydration and nutrition from a PVS patient. Irish courts would almost certainly require court approval to be sought in these situations and might also require court approval in a much wider range of circumstances. For example, is court consent required for a girl with an intellectual disability to receive the injectible contraceptive Depo-Provera? Does corrective dental surgery require court permission? The simple and deeply unsatisfactory answer is that we do not know.

The Mental Health Act 2001

In the legal vacuum set out above, the Mental Health Act 2001 does provide limited guidance in relation to some aspects of consent. The Act applies only to people suffering from a 'mental disorder' and to the provision of treatment aimed at ameliorating this disorder. A mental disorder is defined as 'a mental illness, severe dementia or significant intellectual disability' where either there is a serious likelihood of the person causing immediate and serious harm to himself or others or where his condition is so serious that the failure to admit him for treatment would be likely to lead to a serious deterioration in his condition.[8] Thus, the Act is concerned primarily with defining the circumstances in which people can be detained for compulsory mental treatment and has little relevance outside of this relatively narrow set of circumstances.

Under the Act, the patient's consent to treatment for a mental disorder must be obtained provided that the patient is 'capable of understanding the nature, purpose and likely effects of the proposed treatment'.[9] Consent, in this context, is defined in a way which approximates quite closely to the ideal of informed consent. It must be obtained freely without threats or inducements. The patient must be given adequate information about the nature, purpose and likely effects of the proposed treatment. This information must be provided in a form and language that the patient can understand. Treatment without consent for a mental disorder may only be given in limited circumstances.[10] Certain treatments have specified additional requirements. Psycho-surgery (any operation which destroys brain tissue) may only be carried out with the patient's consent or the special permission of a Mental Health Tribunal[11] and after the expiration of the time during which an appeal to the Circuit Court may be brought.[12] Electro-convulsive therapy must either have patient consent or be approved by another consultant psychiatrist and used only in accordance with rules drawn up by the Mental Health Commission.[13] Continuing prescribed medicine beyond three months also requires either patient consent or that a second opinion of another consultant psychiatrist be obtained.[14]

The Mental Health Act 2001 is a step in the right direction in providing some measure of protection for people who do not have the capacity to give a personal consent. It is however irrelevant to the majority of people with mental illness, dementia or mental disability whose conditions do not come within the definitions in the Act. Outside of the narrow ambit of the Mental Health Act, the necessary protections are still not in place to protect these vulnerable people from inappropriate medical treatment.

Why Greater Protection is Needed

In addition to the legal uncertainties in the current situation, there are other reasons why greater protection is needed. Current procedures leave little means of detection of inappropriate medical treatment. Many of the people who are not in a position to consent to medical treatment are also not in a position to police their own treatment, to realize if medicines are not working effectively and to communicate their views to their medical advisors. In some circumstances, their families, guardians or carers may not be in a position to adequately police their treatment on their behalf.[15] Inevitably there are problems.

Research on prescribing practices for people with learning disabilities indicates that these people are prescribed very heavy levels of medication, especially anti-psychotic medication, which is used as a means of dealing with 'challenging' behaviour even if the behaviour in question is not as a result of psychiatric illness.[16]

A similar picture emerges in relation to elderly patients, especially those suffering from dementia. The Royal College of Physicians in a report entitled *Medication for Older People* (1997)[17] found that elderly people were much more likely than other patients to suffer from over-prescription, prescription of the wrong type of medicine and poor monitoring of side effects and adverse reactions. One Irish study showed that nursing home residents were prescribed an average of four drugs per resident, with 41 per cent of residents taking five or more drugs.[18] One UK study has shown that almost one in five admissions of elderly people to hospital may be because of inappropriate drug therapy.[19] Thus, there is consistent evidence that vulnerable people do receive inappropriate treatment, caused in part at least because of the absence of somebody with the authority to monitor their care.

Greater protection is also needed in order to respect the fundamental human rights of people with impaired mental capacity. Mental incapacity does not diminish an individual's basic human rights, including the individual's right to autonomy. As was acknowledged by Justice O'Flaherty in *In Re a Ward of Court* (1995), any diminution in the rights of a person without mental capacity to make his own decisions would be an invidious discrimination between 'the well and the infirm.'[20] The recognition of these rights requires us to seek out ways to maximize the autonomy of people who cannot make their own medical decisions. However, as with the exercise of parental autonomy (considered in the last chapter), this respect for autonomy must be balanced with a concern for the welfare of the patient. Some of the challenges posed by this balancing task are set out below.

Respecting the Rights of Legally Incompetent Patients

Traditionally, decision-making for mentally incapacitated patients took little cognisance of the need to respect the patient's autonomy. However, as the informed consent doctrine developed in the United States, courts and commentators became increasingly conscious of the need to extend the philosophy behind informed consent even where personal informed consent was impossible. This concern is slowly also taking hold on this side of the Atlantic, although Irish developments in this regard have been limited.

Looking at What the Patient Would Have Wanted

In the United States, when required to make a decision for a legally incompetent patient about what medical treatment should be given or, more frequently, not given or withdrawn, the courts have asked what the individual would have wanted. This form of decision-making is known as 'substituted judgment' and is used by the courts in almost all US states.[21] Asking what the person would have wanted is, on its face, protective of patient autonomy. Rather than deciding what is in the best interests of the patient, the court looks at the patient himself for guidance.

This method of making decisions works best where a person while competent has given clear and unequivocal indications of what kind of treatment he would have wanted. However, outside of this circumstance, it frequently becomes meaningless because the decision-maker simply does not know what the mentally incapacitated patient would have wanted. This may be either because a previously competent individual has not given sufficiently clear instructions to cover the situation in question,[22] or because the individual has never had the capacity to decide.[23]

In other words, although the idea sounds promising, making decisions on the basis of 'substituted judgment', will not, of itself, always protect an incompetent patient's rights.

In Ireland, the Supreme Court in *In Re a Ward of Court* (1995) preferred to look to the woman's best interests rather than to what she would have wanted. However, some of the judges did suggest that the question of what the patient would have wanted must be a necessary component of any decision based on her best interests.[24] This is a good compromise, respecting the patient's autonomy without losing sight of the importance of his best interests.

Alongside the focus on 'substituted judgment', the widespread concern in the US with patient autonomy has led to a flourishing of legislation relating to Advance Directives. 'Living will' and 'enduring power of attorney' statutes are now found on the statute books of almost all the states in the US. A 'living will' enables a competent individual to set out clearly the extent of treatment he wishes to consent to should he become mentally incapacitated. In this way, he can maintain some control over his healthcare decisions even after he has lost mental capacity. The creation of an 'enduring power of attorney' enables a competent person to delegate the power of decision-making to another person in the event of future incompetence. This decision-making power may even extend to allow the representative to make the ultimate decision about when to cease life-saving or life-sustaining treatment. Again, by being able to choose as his representative a person who understands his preferences, the patient has the best chance of having his wishes respected even when he is no longer capable of exercising his own personal control.

In spite of their obvious attractions, living wills and enduring powers of attorney provide only a limited protection of autonomy. In the US, in spite of the widespread legislation and considerable publicity, the vast majority of people do not take the legal steps necessary to exercise this kind of choice. The unpleasantness of facing up to one's mortality is not diminished because of the existence of a legal framework to give effect to one's wishes. There are also important questions about how advance directives should relate to the current welfare of the patient. For example, should the decision of a 25-year-old unmarried man to refuse all life-saving treatment if he were to become mentally incompetent be implemented if he has become a 70-year-old man with a supportive family, mild dementia, a happy disposition and an easily curable condition?[25]

For Irish patients, the option of making any legally recognized advance directive is simply not available. Healthcare decisions are excluded from the scheme of the Enduring Powers of Attorney Act 1996 (which permits a person in full possession of his mental capacity to designate somebody to act on his behalf in the event of future mental incapacity). It is possible that, even though there is no legislative framework in place, a court might in some circumstances recognize a person's advance decision as to how he would wish to be treated. However, the fact that there is no certainty would hardly inspire confidence in a patient faced with, for example, Alzheimer's Disease, who wishes to set his own agenda for the care and treatment he will receive. The failure to include healthcare decisions in the legislation is a clear example of a legislative cop-out. Rather than face the undoubtedly serious and controversial questions to which this kind of legal facility gives rise, the legislature preferred to pretend they did not exist. Given that a rise in instances of dementia is an inevitable consequence of our ageing population, this is an unacceptable abrogation of legislative responsibility.

Looking at What the Patient Does Want

Advance decision-making is only of relevance for patients who were once competent and who availed of the facility offered. Outside of this, however, there are still ways in which the autonomy of people who cannot give personal consent can be protected. As recognized by the English Law Commission in its *Report on Mental Incapacity* (1995),[26] just because an individual does not have sufficient legal capacity to give consent on his own behalf does not mean that he cannot have a view on a proposed procedure if this is explained properly to him. Simple steps such as using more accessible language, explaining a proposed procedure in smaller elements and using verbal and non-verbal means of presenting information can have an important impact on an individual's capacity to participate in the decision-making process.[27] With this in mind, the English Law Commission has recommended that any decision about an individual's best interests must take account of the past and present wishes of the individual and the need to permit and encourage the individual to participate in the decision-making process.[28]

Evaluating Ireland's Legal Position

The Irish legal position relating to medical treatment in the absence of personal consent is simply unacceptable. Our current lack of a proper legal framework fails to protect either the autonomy or the welfare of the patient. It also places doctors in a very difficult position, uncertain about what kinds of treatment they can and cannot provide. Although the Mental Health Act 2001 has begun the process of reforming this area, a more wide-ranging reform is urgently needed. There are useful lessons to be learned from other countries and, in particular, from the English Law Commission's thoughtful and comprehensive *Report on Mental Incapacity* (1995). This report has been endorsed by the British Government, which has promised to bring forward substantial new legislation in this area.[29] The Scottish Parliament has already done this and the Adults with Incapacity (Scotland) Act 2000 was one of the first Acts of the new Scottish parliment.[30] It is time for Irish legislators to think about following suit.

8. Conclusion: Bridging the Gap

In a survey of public priorities carried out in August 2001, 95 per cent of people surveyed regarded healthcare as the most important priority within the National Development Plan.[1] All the main political parties have placed healthcare reform at the top of their agendas. The new government has promised to deliver an improved healthcare system. It is in this context that, in November 2001, the Department of Health and Children published its health strategy entitled *Quality and Fairness: A Health System for You*. This strategy sets out the Department's plans for the development, reform and modernization of the Irish healthcare system over the next decade. A primary objective of the strategy is that the patient be made central in the delivery of healthcare.

In line with the reforming spirit currently abroad, this pamphlet looks at one aspect of our healthcare system, namely, the role of the patient in the delivery of healthcare as viewed through the application of the principle of informed consent. Its argument is that protecting patient autonomy is an important priority which must be given due recognition within our healthcare system. This means that the issues of consent and communication must be prioritized in the strategic planning for the development of our healthcare system. As Jenkins argues:

> The better the quality of communication between doctor and patient before surgery the less likely legal action will follow adverse outcome. Quality here means more than facts. It includes kindness and sympathy. The experience of being a patient is the best way of understanding consent; at the end of the day it is a matter of trust.[2]

Before looking at how to prioritize these issues, it is useful to recall in brief why it is that our current healthcare system has failed to deliver the ideal of informed consent.

Why the Failure to Deliver Informed Consent?

There are a number of reasons for the failure to deliver informed consent. First, the primary means of giving effect to the requirement for informed consent has been the law, and specifically the law of tort. As was seen in Chapter 4, the law of tort is patently unsatisfactory as a means of delivering an ideal as complex and nuanced as informed consent. Tort actions are too antagonistic, too expensive, too demanding and too uncertain to provide patients with a means of enforcing their rights. Most patients do not want to sue their doctors. Instead what they want is to be treated with respect and consideration.

A second reason why consent and communication have not been sufficiently prioritized is because of the many pressures on our underfunded healthcare system. It takes time to listen and explain to patients, and to encourage their questions. In a system stretched towards breaking point, time is frequently in short supply. In our two-tier system, this is especially true for public patients. One surgeon in evidence to the Bristol Inquiry described his approach (in the context of the NHS) as follows:

> Communication is an expensive luxury. I have never yet had a complaint from one of my private patients because in my private practice, I have time to handle all aspects of a case.[3]

A third reason for the failure to deliver the ideal of informed consent is the lack of either professional or legal guidance for doctors. In Britain, the General Medical Council issues detailed guidelines dealing exclusively with the question of consent.[4] As was seen in Chapter 3, in Ireland doctors have to rely on the general *Guide to Ethical Conduct and Behaviour* (1998), which is short on specifics on the question of consent. The problems created by the absence of professional guidance is accentuated by the lack of legal certainty in relation to many important issues. Thus, as discussed in Chapter 5, the legal position relating to determinations of competence is unclear and as seen in Chapters 6 and 7, there is also a lack of clarity in relation to the treatment of children and adults who cannot give personal consent. One cannot require doctors to comply with complex legal standards when even lawyers do not know what those standards are.

Delivering the Ideal: Strategic Planning for Consent

A primary objective of the Health Strategy 2001 is that the patient be placed at the centre in the delivery of care. However, the document is short on specifics as regards how this should be done. In brief, the strategy promises the development of a statutory framework to deal with customer complaints, which although not specifically stated, would presumably include complaints in relation to informed consent. The strategy also promises that communication skills will be strengthened through training programmes made available to medical professionals and that professional bodies will be asked to devise codes of practice in order to facilitate shared decision-making. The development of new ways of informing patients is also facilitated and the promised Health Information and Quality Authority is charged with examining the introduction of computer based 'decision aids' aimed at providing an interactive approach to transmitting information to patients.[5]

In so far as they go, the promises contained in the Health Strategy in relation to informed consent and patient participation are positive. It is good to see an acknowledgement of the importance of communication skills training and the recognition of the informational opportunities provided by the Internet and other computer based facilities. However, this recognition must be matched with an appropriate allocation of resources. Communication training has now become a feature of most undergraduate medical degree programmes in Ireland.[6] This kind of training is valuable, but also resource intensive.[7] Training facilities of this kind need to be available not just for trainee doctors but also for medical professionals in practice who wish or need to improve their skills in this important area. Appropriate resources must also be devoted to the development of what the Health Strategy refers to as 'decision aids'. Videos, leaflets, tapes, CDs and Internet resources can all make a contribution to better patient understanding. Once again, these facilities are, at least in the start-up stage, resource intensive. Further research is also needed to understand the best ways of communicating with patients. A recent study carried out at University College, Cork showed that patients responded very positively to a pilot study where they received a letter from their consultant summarizing the key elements from their consultation.[8] This is the kind of research which must be conducted if innovative and effective means of conveying information are to be developed. Once again, this kind of research costs money.

The most important resource of all in facilitating patient understanding is time. It is extremely difficult for professionals working in an underfunded and understaffed health service to find the time needed to explain, to listen, to explore options and to achieve informed consent. This time can be bought only with strategic investment in healthcare personnel.

Recognising Patients' Rights

The Health Strategy is disappointing in one important respect. The document does not specifically propose any greater recognition of patients' rights, but rather talks in terms of a generalized complaints system. It proposes the development of a statutory framework for complaints and promises that the necessary legislation will be prepared by the Department of Health and Children. In this regard, the Strategy fails to recognize that a complaints system provides only one component, albeit an essential one, in the provision of patient-centred care. Most patients do not want to have to complain, rather they want to be treated with respect and dignity. Recognizing the rights of all patients, including children and mentally incapacitated adults, must be an essential feature of delivering the objective of placing the patient at the centre in the delivery of care.

Giving specific recognition to patient rights is important for a number of reasons. First, in spite of the efforts of many in the medical profession, the aim of achieving patient participation will not be achieved solely through the goodwill of the profession. Even if most doctors do work towards the ideal, some vestiges of old-style medical paternalism will inevitably remain unless there is a strong recognition of the inappropriateness of this kind of behaviour. Patients, too, need more concrete confirmation of their rights. In Ireland today, there is still a sizeable number of patients who do not know that they are entitled to receive information and that the information they receive should make sense to them. Even if they do suspect that they should understand what they are being told, many patients may feel intimidated because they cannot follow the language used or because the person conveying the information has made it clear that she does not have the time to engage in discussion. For these patients, the knowledge that they have rights, including a right to information in a form they understand, may provide the impetus they need in order to take a more active role in their own healthcare decisions.

For vulnerable patients, such as children, young people and people with dementia, mental illness, or mental disability, the need to have recognized rights is all the more important. The legal protections currently given to these patients and to their carers are inadequate. This does not appear to be recognized within the Health Strategy. Although recognizing that issues relating to mental health will be a major focus for healthcare in the coming century, the Strategy appears to believe that, from a legal perspective at least, the Department has done all that is necessary. Thus, the primary concern is with implementing the Mental Health Act 2001 and not with developing protections in other regards.

The introduction of a legally recognized and enforceable charter of patients' rights, applicable to all patients, would have both practical and symbolic force. An example of such a charter is New Zealand's *Code of Health and Disability Services Consumers' Rights* (1996).[9] A brief look at how this code operates may indicate how the complaints procedure promised by the Health Strategy could develop if the necessary political will is present. The code, which refers to 'consumers' of healthcare services rather than patients, sets out ten rights accorded to consumers. Among these rights are the right to respect; the right to effective communication; the right to be fully informed; and the right to make an informed choice and to give informed consent. The existence of these rights imposes corresponding duties on healthcare and disability service providers. They must take reasonable actions in the circumstances to give effect to the consumers' rights.[10] The code has legislative backing[11] and consumers can make complaints to the Health and Disability Commissioner. The Commissioner's function is to ensure 'low-level dispute resolution' wherever possible, by facilitating service providers and consumers in discussing the problem and seeking a quick resolution.

The system is not just complaints based. As well as setting out rights for all consumers, the code sets out guidelines for dealing with consumers who do not have the competence to give personal consent. In this way, it performs the important function of giving healthcare providers an indication of the para-meters that should govern decisions in this regard. Under the code, a service may be provided to a consumer where this service is in the best interests of the consumer and reasonable steps have been taken to ascertain the views of the consumer or, if her views cannot be ascertained, of people who are interested in her welfare. The code as operated also plays an educative role. Thus, the Commissioner has delivered a substantial body of Opinions, which give healthcare providers an indication of acceptable practice in specified areas that serve to inform not just healthcare providers but also consumers.[12]

The New Zealand code is just one example of how a legally enforceable charter of rights for patients might operate. There are many other examples. Most European countries and most states in the United States have introduced legally enforceable charters of rights for patients.[13] It is time for Ireland to do the same. Setting up a proper system that can hear complaints and also develop patients' rights will take time and thought. In New Zealand, it took six years from the suggestion that an enforce-able charter of rights be introduced to the final passage of the legislation and it then took a further two years for the code itself to be drawn up. In this context, the promise in the Health Strategy that a complaints system can be set up by the end of 2002 is perhaps a little overly optimistic. The issues at stake are complex ones that must be dealt with in a way that is meaningful for patients while also being fair to medical professionals. Given the current priority of healthcare reform, it is now time to take a step on this road.

Notes and References

INTRODUCTION

1   The Hippocratic Oath is the best known of Hippocrates' prolific writings on ethics and the medical profession. Although in the public's mind, the Oath is closely associated with the medical profession, most doctors no longer take the Oath in its original form. See further *Hippocrates*, 4 vols. (Harvard University Press, 1923–31).

2   For convenience, I use female and male pronouns in alternate chapters when referring to both doctors and patients.

3   Department of Health and Children (Stationery Office, 2001), p. 80. Available at www.doh.ie

4   In January 2000, an inquiry into the practices at the major Irish hospitals in this regard was approved by the Minister for Health and Children. The inquiry, chaired by Anne Dunne, published its interpretation of its terms of reference in March 2001 and confirmed that it hoped to conclude the inquiry and report to the Minister within eighteen months. In July 2001, the inquiry wrote to all the major hospitals in the State, seeking their records relating to all relevant post mortems over the past 30 years. The hospitals indicated at that time that compliance with this request might take up to two years.

5   *North Western Health Board* v *HW and CW* (2001), Unreported Supreme Court, 8 November 2001.

1. DEVELOPING A CULTURE OF CONSENT

1   See the *Irish Times,* 15 February 2001. All the references to the *Irish Times* may be accessed through the *Irish Times* Archive accessible at http://ireland.com

2   See the *Irish Times,* 26 July 2001.

3   The term 'feeble-minded' probably approximates to mildly mentally disabled. The division of people with intellectual disability into 'feeble-minded', 'idiot' and 'imbecile' in descending levels of disability is clearly offensive and inappropriate. Nonetheless, this nomenclature survives in Irish legislation (see section 4 of the Criminal Law Amendment Act 1935).

4   Carrie Buck's daughter was 1-year-old when she was described as being 'of defective mentality', solely on the basis of evidence from one nurse at the institution. When she began to attend school, it became

clear that she had above average intelligence and she performed exceptionally well. Sadly, she died in a fire while still a child.

5   (1927) 274 US 200, 207–8.

6   See Burgdorf and Burgdorf, 'The Wicked Witch is Almost Dead: *Buck* v *Bell* and the Sterilization of Handicapped Persons' (1977), 50 *Temple Law Quarterly* 995 for a detailed history of compulsory sterilization in the United States.

7   The issue came to prominence when details were published in the Swedish newspaper *Dagens Nyheter* in 1997. See the *Irish Times*, 30 August 1997.

8   [1954] IR 73, 87.

9   A close contender for this title is a study into cervical cancer carried out at the National Women's Hospital in Auckland between 1966 and the mid-1970s. Widely known in New Zealand as the 'Unfortunate Experiment', this study saw women (mainly from a lower socio-economic class) who were diagnosed with cervical cancer left untreated in order to observe the natural progression of the disease. As a result of being denied treatment, a number of women lost their lives. In 1988, Judge Sylvia Cartwright chaired a Commission of Inquiry into the experiment and concluded that the study was unethical and should never have received approval.

10   See Katz, Jay, *Experimentation with Human Beings* (New York: Russel Sage Foundation, 1972), for details of these atrocities.

11   For a history of the Tuskagee Syphilis Project, see James H. Jones, *Bad Blood* (New York: Free Press, 1981); a useful summary may be found at http://www.med.virginia.edu/hs-library/historical/apology/report.html

12   *Report on Three Trials Involving Babies and Children in Institutional Settings 1960/61, 1970 and 1973* (Department of Health).

13   See the *Irish Times*, 10 November 2000.

14   Some of the 58 subjects in the first trial (all of whom were resident in children's homes) may have been given a slightly reduced level of protection against the illnesses in question. This trial compared the effects of a polio vaccine given in combination with the DTPP vaccine (commonly known as the three-in-one vaccine – a combination which was the method of vaccination used in Canada and the USA at this time) or the vaccine given separately from, but at the same time as, the DTPP vaccine. A total of 24 infants were given the quadruple vaccine and 28 were given the triple vaccine and the

separate polio vaccine. The results of the first trial on the quadruple vaccine indicated that these children were less satisfactorily protected than those vaccinated with the triple vaccine and the separate polio vaccine. Six months after the initial vaccination, a booster dose vaccine was given to 36 of the children but the others, some of whom had received the less effective vaccine, had left the children's home at this time, were not traced and did not receive the booster. These children were not available for follow-up examination.

15 (1767) 2 Wils K.B. 359, 361.

16 (1914) 211 N.Y. 125, 128.

17 The term 'assault', as used by Justice Cardozo, is a generic term, incorporating the torts of assault and battery. Strictly speaking, medical interventions without consent come within the category of battery.

18 [1995] 2 ILRM 401, 431.

19 The Canadian case of *Murray* v *McMurchy* (1949) 2 D.L.R. 442 is one of the relatively few examples of a successful battery action. Here, the defendant surgeon discovered fibroid tumours in the uterus wall of the plaintiff in the course of a Caesarean section. After consultation with a second surgeon, he performed a sterilization by removing the plaintiff's fallopian tubes to prevent the hazards of a second pregnancy. He was held liable in battery for proceeding with the operation without the consent of the patient.

20 (1957) 317 P 2d 170, 181.

21 (1972) 464 F 2d 772, 780.

22 ibid., 789.

2. THE PRINCIPLES UNDERPINNING CONSENT

1 It is often attributed most directly to the work of the German philosopher, Immanuel Kant. See 'Lectures on Ethics' in Paton, Herbert J. (trans.), *Groundwork of the Metaphysics of Morals* (London: Hutchinson, 1953). See also J.S. Mill 'On Liberty' in *Three Essays* (Oxford University Press, 1972).

2 The term PVS was first coined by Jennett, B. and Plum, F. 'Persistent Vegetative State After Brain Damage' (1972), *The Lancet* 734. Martyn, Susan R. and Bourguignon, Henry 'Coming to Terms With Death' (1991), 42 *Hastings Law Journal*, 817, 819, provide the following summary of the effect of the persistent vegetative state. 'Patients in persistent vegetative state (PVS) can breathe, digest food, and

eliminate waste. They can open and close their eyes, suggesting periods of sleep and waking. They can move their eyes and manifest other reflex responses to external stimuli, such as coughing, gagging, or moving their limbs. But these patients, though occasionally appearing to give conscious responses, do not feel pain or sense their surroundings. They have irretrievably lost consciousness.' However, as noted by Mason, Kenyon, and McCall Smith, Alexander, *Law and Medical Ethics*, 5th edn, (Butterworths, 1999) pp. 394–395 'it is notoriously difficult to identify a satisfactory definition' of the state.

3   Her condition was described by the trial judge as follows: 'She is spastic as a result of the brain damage. Both arms and hands are contracted. Both legs and feet are extended. Her jaws are clenched and because she had a tendency to bite the insides of her cheeks and her tongue, her back teeth have been capped to prevent the front teeth from fully closing. She cannot swallow. She cannot speak. She is incontinent.' Unlike a patient in a fully PVS, however, she may have retained some minimal cognitive capacity. According to the trial judge, if this were the case, the woman's catastrophic situation would be a terrible torment to her and would make her situation worse than if she were fully PVS.

4   *Four Essays on Liberty* (Oxford University Press, 1969), p. 131.

5   *The Theory and Practice of Autonomy* (Cambridge University Press, 1988), p. 21.

6   ibid., p. 48.

7   ibid., p. 32.

8   ibid., pp. 108–9.

9   Schneider, C., *The Practice of Autonomy* (Oxford University Press, 1998), p. 41.

10   Faulder, Carolyn, *Whose Body Is It? The Troubling Issue of Informed Consent* (Virago, 1985).

11   Meredith, Catherine, *et al.,* 'Information needs of cancer patients in west Scotland: cross-sectional survey of patients' views' (1996), 313 *BMJ* 724.

12   See Ajaj, A., Singh M.P., and Abdullah, A.J.J., 'Should Elderly Patients Be Told They Have Cancer? Questionnaire Survey of Older People' (2001), 323 *BMJ* 1160.

13   See Schulman, K., 'Active Patient Orientation and Outcomes in Hypertensive Treatment' (1979), 17 *Med Care* 267.

14 See Fallowfield, Lesley *et al.*, 'Psychological Outcomes of Different Treatment Policies in Women With Early Breast Cancer Outside a Clinical Trial' (1990), 301 *BMJ* 575.

15 See Kaplan, Robert, 'Health-Related Quality of Life in Patient Decision Making' (1991), 47 *Journal of Social Issues* 69.

16 See the Criminal Law (Suicide) Act 1993, section 2 (2) of which provides that a person who aids, abets, counsels or procures the suicide of another is guilty of a criminal offence and is liable to up to 14 years' imprisonment. This Act (and all legislation referred to in this pamphlet) may be accessed at www.bailii.org

17 The circumstances in which a pregnancy may be terminated are set out in the decision in *Attorney General* v *X* [1992] 1 IR 1 which interprets Article 40.3.3 of the Irish Constitution. In brief, a pregnancy may be terminated if there is a real and substantial risk to the life of the mother including a risk arising from suicide. The Twenty-fifth Amendment of the Constitution (Protection of Human Life in Pregnancy) Bill, 2001 had proposed to remove the risk of suicide from the grounds on which a pregnancy may be terminated. In March 2002, this proposal was rejected in a constitutional refendum.

18 See the Health Act 1947 as implemented by a range of Infectious Diseases Regulations.

19 The English and American courts have held in favour of the woman's right to autonomy in these circumstances. See *St George's Healthcare NHS Trust* v *S* [1998] 3 WLR 936 and *Re AC* (1990) 573 A 2d 1253 respectively.

20 op.cit., p. 132.

3. INFORMED CONSENT: THE IDEAL AND THE REALITY

1 See discussion in Chapter 1.

2 See Faden, R., and Beauchamp, T., *A History and Theory of Informed Consent* (Oxford University Press, 1986), Chapter 8.

3 Beauchamp, T., 'Informed Consent' in Veatch, Robert (ed.), *Medical Ethics*, 2nd edn, (Jones and Bartlett, 1997), p. 194.

4 op.cit., p. 300–2.

5 In one study of cancer patients (Cassileth, Barrie R. *et al.*, 'Informed Consent – Why are its Goals Imperfectly Realized?' (1980) 302 *New England Journal of Medicine* 896), 28 per cent of patients believed that, if a patient was given a consent form he had to sign it. Another study of patients admitted to an emergency centre (Boisaubin,

Eugene and Dresser, Rebecca, 'Informed Consent in Emergency Care: Illusion and Reform' (1987) 16 *Annals of Emergency Medicine* 62) showed that few of the patients knew that they had authority to make treatment decisions or the purpose of the consent form signed upon admission.

6   In a major survey of 805 physicians and 1,251 members of the public (Harris, Lou *et al.*, 'Views of Informed Consent and Decisionmaking: Parallel Surveys of Physicians and the Public', in President's Commission *Making Healthcare Decisions* Vol. 2, 17 (Washington: Official Publication, 1982), p. 150) it emerged that while 43 per cent of the public associated the term 'informed consent' with permission or consent to treatment, only 26 per cent of physicians did.

7   See Faden, R., and Beauchamp, T., op.cit., p. 302 (original emphasis).

8   In Harris' study (op.cit., p. 150), 43 per cent of the public and 58 per cent of doctors described informed consent as informing patients about their condition and recommending treatment.

9   Faden, R., and Beauchamp, T., op.cit., p. 308.

10   See Harris (op. cit., p. 123) (94 per cent of patients want their doctor to tell them everything about their condition); O'Flynn, Norma *et al*, 'Consent and Confidentiality in Teaching in General Practice: Survey of Patients' Views on Presence of Students' (1997), 315 *BMJ* 1142 (95 per cent of patients have no objection to students' presence but wished to have their consent sought). See also the surveys cited in Chapter 2 (Meredith *et.al.*, and Ajaj, Singh and Abdullah).

11   op.cit., p. 303 (emphasis added).

12   op.cit., p. 161 (taken from Imbus, S.H. and Zawacki, B.E. 'Autonomy for Burned Patients When Survival is Unprecedented' (1977) 297 *New England Journal of Medicine* 308). Schneider notes the pride with which the unit's medical professionals reported this practice.

13   *Hippocratic Writings*, Chadwick, J. and Mann, W.N. (trans.) (London: Penguin Books, 1950).

14   5th edn, 1998. Copies are available from the Office of the Medical Council but unfortunately at the time of writing it is not available at the Medical Council website (www.medicalcouncil.ie).

15   Benson, John and Britten, Nicky, 'Respecting the Autonomy of Cancer Patients when Talking with their Families: Qualitative Analysis of Semi-structured Interviews with Patients' (1996), 313 *BMJ* 729.

16   Available at www.isqh.net. The survey is considered further below.

17   Taken from Schneider, C., *The Practice of Autonomy*, op.cit., p. 152.

18   'Consent: A Matter of Trust Not Tort' (1996), *Medico-Legal Journal of Ireland* 83, 85.

19   See further Faden, R., and Beauchamp, T., op.cit., Chapter 10.

20   The Department of Health and Children does provide photocopies of the Charter on request (although a little prodding can be required) and at the time of writing the only on-line copy of the Charter is available at the site of Cuidiú: The Irish Childbirth Trust (www.cuidiu-ict.ie/maternity/chart.html).

21   The *Guide* is not a piece of legislation and as such is not legally binding. However, the 'teeth' in the *Guide* are found through the fitness to practice procedures set up under the Medical Practitioners Act 1978. Under section 46 of the Act, if a doctor is found guilty of professional misconduct, he may lose his licence to practice medicine. Oddly, the term 'professional misconduct' is not defined in the Act and one has to look to the non-legal *Guide* to find any definition. The *Guide* defines professional misconduct as 'conduct which doctors of experience, competence and good repute, upholding the fundamental aims of the profession, consider disgraceful and dishonourable'.

22   However, in relation to one aspect of life-sustaining treatment, the *Guide* adopts a position which is clearly contrary to that of the Supreme Court in *In Re a Ward of Court* (1995) by stating that: 'The Council reiterates its view that access to nutrition and hydration remain one of the basic needs of human beings, and all reasonable and practical efforts should be made to maintain both of them.'

23   One form (which, to be fair, is in the process of revision) simply states 'I [name] of [address] hereby consent to undergo [treatment] the nature and effect of which has been explained to me by Dr [name].' Perhaps indicatively, this form was made available only following a request under the Freedom of Information Act 1997.

24   'Learning from Bristol: The Report of the Public Inquiry Into Children's Heart Surgery at the Bristol Royal Infirmary 1984–1995' (2001, Cm 5297(1)). Available at www.bristol-inquiry.org.uk/final_report/

25   ibid., p. 295.

26   See Bergler, J. *et al.*, 'Informed Consent: How Much Does the Patient Understand?' (1980), 27 *Clinical Pharmacology and Therapeutics* 435 (patients did not understand basic terms used in the consent form);

Byrne, P. *et al.*, 'How Informed is Signed Consent? (1988) 296 *British Medical Journal* 839 (out of 100 patients who had given signed consent to surgery two to five days previously, 27 did not know which organ had been operated on and 44 did not know the exact nature of the procedure); Cassileth, Barrie R. *et al.*, 'Informed Consent – Why are its Goals Imperfectly Realized' (1980), 302 *New England Journal of Medicine* 896 (within one day of giving written consent to chemotherapy, a substantial portion of 200 cancer patients could not recall relevant information).

27   The survey was conducted on behalf of the Irish Society for Quality in Healthcare by Anne-Marie Brooks. At the time of writing it is available at www.isqh.net

28   ibid., Table 7.

29   ibid., Table 10.

30   ibid., Table 10.

31   For a summary of findings, see Bruster, Stephen *et al.*, 'National Survey of Hospital Patients' (1994), 309 *BMJ* 1542.

32   See the many surveys cited in Sugarman, Jeremy *et al.*, 'Empirical Research in Informed Consent: An Annotated Bibliography', *Hastings Center Report*, Special Supplement Jan–Feb 1999.

4. DELIVERING CONSENT: THE ROLE OF LAW

 1   Directive 2001/20/EC on the approximation of the laws, regulations and administrative procedures of the Member States relating to the implementation of good clinical practice in the conduct of clinical trials on medicinal products for human use.

 2   ibid., section 9 (4).

 3   ibid., section 9 (5) and 9 (6).

 4   ibid., section 9 (7) (a).

 5   ibid., section 9 (7) (b).

 6   There is a general provision (section 9 [4] [e]) enabling the Minister to make general regulations setting out additional matters that should be drawn to the participant's attention or to require specific disclosures in an individual case.

 7   The Act is also extraordinary in that section 6 (b) of the Act excludes from its ambit clinical trials where the tested substance is to be administered to medical, dental or pharmacy students 'as part of . . . a course of training'. Given that students are *more* likely to be vulnerable in relation to clinical trials, this exclusion is baffling.

8   These rights are not specifically enumerated in the Constitution. However, they are among the 'personal rights' guaranteed by Article 40.3.1 of the Constitution (see *In Re a Ward of Court* [1995] 2 ILRM 401).

9   *Walsh* v *Family Planning Services* [1992] 1 IR 496, 504.

10   ibid., 522.

11   The seminal article is by McCoid, Allan H., 'A Reappraisal of Liability for Unauthorised Treatment' (1957), 41 *Minn Law Rev* 381.

12   See the Canadian case of *Reibl* v *Hughes* (1980) 114 DLR (3d) 1, and the Irish case of *Walsh* v *Family Planning Services* [1992], 1 IR 496.

13   See *Sidaway* v *Board of Governors of the Bethlem Royal Hospital* [1985], AC 871.

14   Katz, Jay, *The Silent World of Doctor and Patient*, (The Free Press, 1984), p. 83.

15   *Haughian* v *Paine* (1987) 37 DLR (4th) 624 (Sask CA). See also the Californian case of *Cobbs* v *Grant* (1972) 8 Cal 2d 229.

16   *Faya and Rossi* v *Almaraz* (1993) 620 A 2d 327.

17   (1990) 51 Cal 3d 120 (Cal Sup Ct).

18   *Arato* v *Avendon* (1993) 858 P 2d 598.

19   An attempt was made in *Walsh* v *Family Planning Services* (1992). Here, the claimant argued that his consent had not been valid because the performing surgeon had been assisted by a third party without the claimant's prior consent. The Supreme Court rejected this argument, holding ([1992] 1 IR 496, 530–531) that 'what the patient was agreeing to was that the operation should be carried out by a person or persons with the requisite skill and that it should be competently done'. However, the Court did not close the door completely on these kinds of actions. It noted that when Mr Walsh had consented to the operation, he was not aware of the competence of the performing surgeon. This suggests that a court might take a different approach if a particular surgeon has been specially chosen by a patient because of the patient's faith in that surgeon's ability.

20   One exception is a rather oblique comment by Justice O'Flaherty in *Walsh* v *Family Planning Services* [1992] 1 IR 496, 534–5, that the patient should have been made 'to appreciate fully what was in store for him'.

5. COMPETENT TO CONSENT

1   See Gunn, Michael *et al.*, 'Decision Making Capacity' (1999), 7 *Medical Law Review* 269.

2   'Surgical, medical or dental treatment' is defined in s 23 (2) as including 'any procedure undertaken for the purposes of diagnosis'. The section also applies to 'any procedure (including in particular the administration of an anaesthetic) which is ancillary to any treatment as it applies to that treatment'.

3   See *Gillick* v *West Norfolk and Wisbech A.H.A* [1986]) A.C. 112, 189.

4   Two of the five members of the House of Lords regarded contraceptive treatment as raising specific issues because sexual intercourse below the age of 16 was a criminal offence, which, they argued, would be facilitated by the provision of access to contraceptive treatment.

5   [1986] A.C. 112, 189.

6   See *Re R (A Minor) (Wardship: Consent to Medical Treatment)* [1991] 4 All ER 177 and *Re W (A Minor) (Medical Treatment)* [1992] 4 All ER 627.

7   See section 56 (a) of the Mental Health Act 2001.

8   See section 2 of the Mental Health Act 2001.

9   The Medical Council's *Guide to Ethical Conduct and Behaviour*, 5th edn, (1998), p. 36, under the heading 'The Mentally Ill', simply states 'If the doctor is in any doubt as to the patient's capacity to consent it is advisable to seek specialist opinion as well as discussing the matter with parents, guardians, or relatives.' Under the heading 'The Mentally Handicapped', it provides that 'The doctor should attempt to obtain consent but, depending on the degree of handicap, may have to consult with the patient's parents or guardians, and, in particularly difficult cases to obtain a second opinion.'

10 These are accessible at http://www.rcpsych.ac.uk/publications/. These guidelines incorporate the guidelines drawn up by the British Medical Association in conjunction with the English Law Society on *Capacity to Consent to and Refuse Medical Treatment* (1995), accessible at www.bma.org.uk/public/ethics.nsf

11 The application of the test led to the opposite conclusion in *Re MB (an adult: medical treatment)* (1997) 38 *BMLR* 175, where the Court of Appeal held that a woman who refused to consent to a Caesarean section because of her dislike of needles was not competent to refuse her consent. The Court considered that her panic fear of needles dominated everything and made her temporarily incompetent.

12 For example, in the American case of *State of Tennessee* v *Northern* (1978) 563 SW 2d 197, the patient refused to believe that her black and withered leg indicated that she had gangrene.

6. DECIDING FOR CHILDREN

1   'People Like That Are the Only People Here', in *Birds of America* (Faber and Faber, 1998), p. 220.

2   Beauchamp, T., 'Informed Consent' in Veatch, Robert (ed.), *Medical Ethics* 2nd edn, (Jones and Bartlett, 1997), p. 194.

3   While 'the Family' has been interpreted to mean a family based on marriage (see *State [Nicolau]* v *An Bord Uchtála* [1966] IR 567), there is no similar requirement in relation to 'parents'.

4   See the *Irish Times,* 3 March 2000.

5   The section allows the Gardaí to take a child into immediate care if they have reasonable grounds for believing that there is a serious and immediate risk to the health or welfare of the child.

6   In *Re T (a minor) (medical treatment)* [1997] 1 WLR 242, the Court of Appeal refused to override the decision of parents to refuse to consent to a life-saving liver transplant operation for their young son. This was in spite of the fact that all the medical evidence indicated that the child would die without the transplant and that he had a good chance of survival with the operation. The Court accorded a great deal of weight to the fact that the parents were 'healthcare professionals' and to the boy's need for ongoing intensive care, which the mother would find difficult (especially as the child's father now lived abroad).

7   Unreported High Court, 27 October 2000, at p. 14 of the transcript. See further Martin, F., 'Parental Rights to Withhold Consent to Medical Treatment for their Child: A Conflict of Rights?' (2001), 7 *Irish Law Times* 114.

8   The decision would almost certainly make it impossible to introduce a compulsory vaccination programme for some childhood illnesses, such as operates in a number of European countries and the USA (where it operates as the 'no shots, no school' programme). In 2000, only 80 per cent of Irish children took the MMR vaccine while only 86 per cent took the HIB vaccine. This is, on average, 10 per cent less than the take-up in Northern Ireland. The low take-up rate is, in part, attributable to the much publicized but scientifically disputed attribution of a connection between certain vaccines and the development of autism. See the Oireachtas Joint Committee on Health and Children *Report on Childhood Immunisation 2001* (accessible at www.gov.ie/oireachtas) which recommends the provision of accurate and accessible information (including

information about numbers of adverse reactions and ongoing research into any connection with autism) in order to enable parents to make an informed choice.

9   'Learning from Bristol: The Report of the Public Inquiry Into Children's Heart Surgery at the Bristol Royal Infirmary 1984–1995 (2001, Cm 5297 (1)) p. 295. Available at www.bristol-inquiry.org.uk/final_report/. The investigation into practices relating to children's heart surgery as carried out at the Bristol Royal Infirmary was the most extensive inquiry ever undertaken into the British NHS. The inquiry lasted two and a half years and took evidence from 577 witnesses, including 238 parents. The report is based on 96 days of oral evidence and 900,000 pages of documents.

10   ibid., p. 1.

11   ibid., p. 219.

12   ibid., p. 282.

13   ibid., p. 219.

14   ibid., p. 284 *et seq.*

15   This is in line with the UN Convention on the Rights of the Child (1989) which requires that 'the child who is capable of forming his or her own views [be accorded] the right to express those views freely in all matters affecting the child, the views of the child being given due weight in accordance with the age and maturity of the child.'

7. DECIDING FOR ADULTS

1   Fantasy Films/United Artists, directed by Milos Forman (1975).

2   The age of majority under the Age of Majority Act 1985.

3   See *Holmes* v *Heatley* (1937) 3 Ir Jur Reports 74.

4   See section 9 (1) of the Courts (Supplemental Provisions) Act, 1961.

5   For the specific wording of the *Guide* on this matter, see Chapter 5, note 9.

6   *Re F (Mental Patient: Sterilization)* [1990] 2 A.C. 1.

7   See *Re A (Medical Treatment: Male Sterilization)* [2000] 1 FCR 193.

8   See section 3 of the Mental Health Act 2001.

9   Section 56 of the Mental Health Act 2001 and the discussion in Chapter 5.

10   Section 57 of the Mental Health Act 2001.

11   Mental Health Tribunals are to be constituted in accordance with section 48 of the Act. They will consist of three members – one

consultant psychiatrist, one solicitor or barrister and one lay person – and will be appointed by the Mental Health Commission.

12   Section 58 of the Act.

13   Section 59 of the Act. The Mental Health Commission is established by section 32 of the Act and consists of 13 members which are to be appointed by the Minister for Health and Children in accordance with detailed criteria laid down in section 35 of the Act.

14   Section 60 of the Act.

15   This is especially the case given that, unlike the majority of children, adults in these situations may often not have family members still alive to take an active interest in their medical treatment on their behalf.

16   See Coughlan, B.J., 'Psychopharmacology in the Treatment of People with Learning Disabilities: A Review' (2000), 31 *Mental Healthcare* 304.

17   2nd edn (Royal College of Physicians, 1997).

18   See Nolan, L. and O'Malley, K., 'The Need for a More Rational Approach to Drug Prescribing for Elderly People in Nursing Homes' (1989), 18 *Ann Int Med* 52. Although these figures are high, the US and UK figures are higher still with an average of six to seven drugs per resident prescribed.

19   See Furniss, L., 'Medicines Use in Nursing Homes' (2000), *Primary Care Pharmacy* 125.

20   *In Re a Ward of Court* (1995), 2 ILRM 401, 431. By a majority of four to one, the Supreme Court agreed to the cessation of treatment on the basis of a range of rights, including the right to life, privacy, bodily integrity, choice, autonomy, dignity in life and dignity in death. For a number of these rights (the last four mentioned), this was their first appearance in an Irish constitutional setting.

21   See Harmon L., 'Falling Off the Vine: Legal Fiction and the Doctrine of Substituted Judgment' (1990), 100 *Yale Law Journal* 1; Delaney J., 'Specific Intent: Substituted Judgment and Best Interests: A Nation-wide Analysis of an Individual's Right to Die' (1991), 11 *Pace Law Review* 565.

22   The standard of clarity of intention required is obviously fundamen-tal here. In *Cruzan* v *Harmon* (1988), 760 S.W.2d 408, the Supreme Court of Missouri required clear and convincing evidence of prior intention. In this case, Nancy Cruzan was a 25-year-old woman who

was in a PVS following a car accident. Her parents sought permission to cease hydration and nutrition on the basis that this was what Nancy would have wanted. They referred to a conversation in which Nancy 'expressed thoughts at age twenty-five in somewhat serious conversation with a housemate friend that if sick or injured she would not wish to continue her life unless she could not live at least halfway normally...' The Court held that this was not sufficient evidence of her intention and therefore rejected her parents' application. The right of each State to adopt its own standard of proof in determining prior intention was upheld on appeal by the United States Supreme Court in *Cruzan* v *Director, Missouri Department of Health* (1990) 497 U.S. 261.

23   These difficulties have not always prevented the US courts from applying the test and a number of decisions show courts using 'substituted judgment' to make decisions on behalf of patients with learning difficulties with no evidence whatsoever of what the patient would have wanted. A classic example is found in *Superintendent of Belchertown* v *Saikewicz* 373 Mass. 723; 370 N.E.2d 417 (1977) where the Supreme Judicial Court of Massachusetts used 'substituted judgment' to justify not providing chemotherapy to a 67-year-old man with profound mental disability who had been resident in a State institution for the previous 50 years. In the view of the Court, but with no supporting evidence, although the majority of people would have opted for the chemotherapy, a person in Mr Saikewicz's position (mentally disabled, resident in an institution, unable to understand the pain and discomfort of the treatment etc.) would have not have opted for it.

24   See in particular the judgment of Justice Denham at [1995] 2 ILRM 401, 463.

25   See further the debate between Dresser, R., and Rhoden, N., contained in Dresser, R., 'Life, Death, and Incompetent Patients: Conceptual Infirmities and Hidden Values in the Law' (1986), 28 *Arizona Law Review* 373 and 'Relitigating Life and Death' (1990), 51 *Ohio State Law Journal* 425 and Rhoden, N., 'The Limits of Legal Objectivity' (1990), 68 *NCL Rev* 845 and 'Litigating Life and Death' (1988), 102 *Harv L Rev* 375.

26   Law Com No 231 (HMSO, 1995) at para 3.28.

27   See Gunn, Michael, *et.al.*, 'Decision Making Capacity' (1999), 7 *Medical Law Review* 269.

28   The English courts have, to date, been slow to adopt this participative approach. In *Re A (Medical Treatment: Male Sterilization)* [2000] 1 FCR 193 the Court of Appeal had to decide whether it was in the best interests of a man with Down's syndrome to consent on his behalf to the performance of a vasectomy operation. Even though the Court (quite correctly) refused to give its consent on the basis that the surgery was not in the man's best interests, not one of the three members of the Court gave any weight to the fact that the man had said that he did not want the procedure done.

29   See the Lord Chancellor's Department, *Making Decisions: The Government's Proposals for Making Decisions On Behalf of Mentally Incapacitated Adults Report* (1999). Available at: www.lcd.gov.uk/family/mdecisions/indbod.htm

30   The Act may be accessed at http://www.scotland-legislation.hmsogov.uk

8. CONCLUSION: BRIDGING THE GAP

1   See the *Irish Times,* 23 August, 2001.

2   Jenkins, D., 'Consent: A Matter of Trust Not Tort' (1996), *Medico-Legal Journal of Ireland* 83, p. 83.

3   'Learning from Bristol: The Report of the Public Inquiry Into Children's Heart Surgery at the Bristol Royal Infirmary 1984–1995' (2001, Cm 5297(1)), p. 291.

4   *Seeking Consent: The Ethical Considerations* (November, 1998). These guidelines may be accessed at the GMC's website at www.gmc-uk.org

5   *Quality and Fairness: A Health System for You* (Department of Health and Children, Stationery Office, 2001), p. 80. Available at www.doh.ie

6   One course provided by the Royal College of Surgeons uses videotaping of consultations involving professional actors and former patients to enable doctors in training to simulate real-life situations. The course was profiled in the *Irish Times,* 21 February 2000 under the rather unfortunate heading 'Charm School for Doctors'.

7   This point was aptly made by Professor Colin Bradley, Professor of General Practice at University College, Cork in a letter to the *Irish Times,* 24 February 2000.

8   Ninety per cent of the patients said they were either very pleased or pleased to get the letter. However, only 60 per cent said that they understood all of the letter. These findings were presented to the Annual Conference of the Health Promoting Hospitals Network. See the *Irish Medical News* 22 October 2001.

9   The impetus for the Code comes from New Zealand's own experi-
    ence of blatant disregard for patient consent, the details of which are
    discussed in Chapter 1, note 9. Among the recommendations made
    following the public inquiry was the establishment of an office or
    body to define, monitor and protect patients' rights.

10 A full copy of the code as well as further details about the legislation
    and the office of Health and Disability Commissioner may be obtained
    at www.hdc.org.nz

11 See the Health and Disability Commissioner Act 1994.

12 These are also available at www.hdc.org.nz

13 A (slightly out-of-date) summary of the status of patients' rights
    throughout the world may be found at: www.consumersinterna-
    tional.org/campaigns/patientsrights/activities.html

Table of Cases

Bibliography

Ajaj, A, Singh, M.P. and Abdullah, A.J.J., 'Should Elderly Patients Be Told They Have Cancer? Questionnaire Survey of Older People' (2001), 323 *British Medical Journal* 1160

Annas, George, *Some Choice: Law, Medicine and the Market* (Oxford University Press, 1998)

Benson, John and Britten, Nicky, 'Respecting the Autonomy of Cancer Patients when Talking with their Families: Qualitative Analysis of Semi-structured Interviews with Patients' (1996), 313 *British Medical Journal* 729

Bergler, J. *et al.*, 'Informed Consent: How Much Does the Patient Understand?' (1980), 27 *Clinical Pharmacology and Therapeutics* 435

Berlin, Isaiah, *Four Essays on Liberty* (Oxford University Press, 1969)

Boisaubin, Eugene B. and Dresser, Rebecca, 'Informed Consent in Emergency Care: Illusion and Reform' (1987), 16 *Annals of Emergency Medicine* 62

Brazier, Margaret and Bridge, Caroline, 'Coercion or Caring: Analysing Adolescent Autonomy' (1996), 16 *Legal Studies* 84

Bruster, Stephen, *et al.*, 'National survey of Hospital Patients' (1994), 309 *British Medical Journal* 1542

Buchanan, Allen and Brock, Dan, *Deciding for Others: The Ethics of Surrogate Decision Making* (Cambridge University Press, 1989)

Burgdorf, Robert L. and Burgdorf, Marcia Pearce, 'The Wicked Witch is Almost Dead: *Buck* v *Bell* and the Sterilisation of Handicapped Persons' (1977), 50 *Temple Law Quarterly* 995

Byrne, P. *et al.*, 'How Informed is Signed Consent?' (1988), 296 *British Medical Journal* 839

Cassileth, Barrie R., *et al.*, 'Informed Consent – Why are its Goals Imperfectly Realized' (1980), 302 *New England Journal of Medicine* 896

Coughlan, Barry J., 'Psychopharmacology in the Treatment of People with Learning Disabilities: A Review' (2000), 31 *Mental Health Care* 304

Delaney, Jeffrey J., 'Specific Intent: Substituted Judgment and Best Interests: A Nationwide Analysis of an Individual's Right to Die' (1991), 11 *Pace Law Review* 565

Donnelly, Mary, 'Capacity of Minors to Consent to Medical and Contraceptive Treatment' (1995), *Medico-Legal Journal of Ireland* 18

Donnelly, Mary, 'Confusion and Uncertainty: The Irish Approach to the

Duty to Disclose Risks in Medical Treatment' (1996), 3 *Medico-Legal Journal of Ireland* 3

Donnelly, Mary, 'The Legality of Non-Consensual Sterilisation of Mentally Disabled People' (1997), 32 *Irish Jurist* 297

Dresser, Rebecca, 'Life, Death, and Incompetent Patients: Conceptual Infirmities and Hidden Values in the Law' (1986), 28 *Arizona Law Review* 373

Dresser, Rebecca, 'Relitigating Life and Death' (1990), 51 *Ohio State Law Journal* 425

Dworkin, Gerald, *The Theory and Practice of Autonomy* (Cambridge University Press, 1988)

Faden, Ruth R. and Beauchamp, Tom L., *A History and Theory of Informed Consent* (Oxford University Press, 1986)

Fallowfield, Lesley *et al.*, 'Psychological Outcomes of Different Treatment Policies in Women With Early Breast Cancer Outside a Clinical Trial' (1990), 301 *British Medical Journal*

Faulder, Carolyn, *Whose Body Is It? The Troubling Issue of Informed Consent* (London: Virago, 1985)

Fox, Marie and McHale, Jean, 'In whose Best Interests?' (1997), 60 *Modern Law Review* 700

Furniss, L., 'Medicines Use in Nursing Homes' (2000), *Primary Care Pharmacy* 125

Grubb, Andrew, 'The Emergence and Rise of Medical Ethics' (1987), 50 *Modern Law Review* 241

Grubb, Andrew (ed.), *Choices and Decisions in Health Care* (Chicester, New York: John Wiley & Sons, 1993)

Gunn, Michael *et al.*, 'Decision Making Capacity' (1999), 7 *Medical Law Review* 269

Harmon, Louise, 'Falling Off the Vine: Legal Fiction and the Doctrine of Substituted Judgment' (1990), 100 *Yale Law Journal* 1

Harris, Lou *et al.*, 'Views of Informed Consent and Decision-making: Parallel Surveys of Physicians and the Public', in President's Commission *Making Healthcare Decisions* Vol. 2, 17 (Washington: Official Publication, 1982)

Healy, John, *Medical Negligence: Common Law Perspectives* (London: Sweet and Maxwell, 2000)

Hillary, Irene *et al.*, 'Antibody Response in Infants to the Polimyelitis Component of a Quadruple Vaccine' (1962), *British Medical Journal*, 1098

Hillary, 'Trials of Intranasally Administered Rubella Vaccine' (1971), 69 *J. Hyg. Camb.* 547

Imbus, S.H. and Zawacki, B.E. 'Autonomy for Burned Patients When Survival is Unprecedented' (1977) 297 *New England Journal of Medicine* 308

Jenkins, David, 'Consent: A Matter of Trust Not Tort' (1996), *Medico-Legal Journal of Ireland* 83

Jennett, B. and Plum, F. 'Persistent Vegetative State After Brain Damage' [1972] *The Lancet* 734

Jones, James H., *Bad Blood* (New York: Free Press, 1981)

Jones, Michael, and Keywood, Kirsty, 'Assessing the Patient's Competence to Consent to Medical Treatment' (1996), 2 *Medical Law International* 107

Kaplan, Robert, 'Health-Related Quality of Life in Patient Decision Making' (1991), 47 *Journal of Social Issues* 69

Katz, Jay, *Experimentation with Human Beings* (New York: Russell Sage Foundation, 1972)

Katz, Jay, *The Silent World of Doctor and Patient* (New York: Free Press, 1984)

Kilkelly, Ursula, *The Child and the European Convention on Human Rights* (Dartmouth: Ashgate, 1999)

Martin, Frank, 'Parental Rights to Withhold Consent to Medical Treatment for their Child: A Conflict of Rights?' (2001), 7 *Irish Law Times* 114

Martyn, Susan R. and Bourguignon, Henry 'Coming to Terms With Death' (1991), 42 *Hastings Law Journal* 817

Mason, J. K. and McCall Smith, Alexander, *Law and Medical Ethics* 5th edn, (London: Butterworths, 1999)

McCoid, Allan H., 'A Reappraisal of Liability for Unauthorised Treatment' (1957), 41 *Minn. Law Review* 381

McMahon, Bryan and Binchy, William, *Law of Torts* 3rd edn, (Dublin: Butterworths, 2000)

Meredith, Catherine *et al.*, 'Information needs of cancer patients in west Scotland: cross-sectional survey of patients' views' (1996), 313 *British Medical Journal* 724

Mill, J.S., 'On Liberty' in *Three Essays* (Oxford University Press, 1972)

O'Flynn, Norma *et al.*, 'Consent and Confidentiality in Teaching in General Practice: Survey of Patients' Views on Presence of Students' (1997), 315 *British Medical Journal* 1142

Nolan, L. and O'Malley, K., 'The Need for a More Rational Approach to Drug Prescribing for Elderly People in Nursing Homes' (1989), 18 *Annals of Internal Medicine* 52

Paton, Herbert J. (trans.), *Groundwork of the Metaphysics of Morals* (London: Hutchinson, 1953).

President's Commission for the Study of Ethical Problems in Medicine and Biomedical and Behaviour Research, *Making Health Care Decisions* (1982)

Report on Three Trials Involving Babies and Children in Institutional Settings 1960/61, 1970 and 1973 (Department of Health, 2000)

Rhoden, Nancy, 'Litigating Life and Death' (1988), 102 *Harvard Law Review* 375

Rhoden, Nancy, 'The Limits of Legal Objectivity' (1990), 68 *North Carolina Law Review* 845

Roth, A. Meisel, L.H. and Lidz, C.W., 'Tests of Competency to Consent to Treatment' (1977), 134 *American Journal of Psychiatry* 279

Schneider, Carl, *The Practice of Autonomy* (Oxford University Press, 1998)

Schulman, K., 'Active Patient Orientation and Outcomes in Hypertensive Treatment' (1979), 17 *Med Care* 267

Sugarman, Jeremy *et al.*, 'Empirical Research in Informed Consent: An Annotated Bibliography', *Hastings Center Report,* Special Supplement, Jan.-Feb. 1999

Teff, Harvey, *Reasonable Care: Legal Perspectives on the Doctor–Patient Relationship* (Oxford: Clarendon Press, 1994)

Veatch, Robert, (ed.), *Medical Ethics*, 2nd edn, (Sudbury, Mass.: Jones and Bartlett, 1997)